Python

- The Bible-
3 Manuscripts in 1 book:

-Python Programming For Beginners

-Python Programming For Intermediates

-Python Programming for Advanced

Python Programming For Beginners

Learn The Basics Of Python In 7 Days!

Maurice J. Thompson

information is without contract or any type of guarantee assurance.

The trademarks that are used are without any consent, and the publication of the trademark is without permission or backing by the trademark owner. All trademarks and brands within this book are for clarifying purposes only and are the owned by the owners themselves, not affiliated with this document.

Table of Contents

Introduction

I want to thank you and congratulate you for buying the book, *"Python Programming For Beginners: Learn The Basics Of Python In 7 Days!"*

This book will help you to understand the basics of python in just 7 days.

Code is the language of the future. And the time to learn the ins and outs of coding is now, unless of course you want to be left behind from the biggest revolution that mankind will witness.

So what does it take to be one of those who the masses will rely on to create products, change them and do a lot more with technology? Well, the secret is in learning programming languages because every electronic device runs on some sort of programming language.

The question then becomes; so which programming language should you at least prioritize to learn given that there are so many programming languages?

Well, if for whatever reason, you have been looking to learn programming or perhaps looking to improve your programming skills, Python programming language could be the best option you can get right now. It makes everything so easy! From the rich and well-designed standard library and built-ins to the availability of modules and numerous third-party open source libraries, very few programming languages can beat it.

Particularly, if you are a beginner who is looking to dip his or her feet into programming, you need to learn a simple language that is easy to understand and that has easy to maintain code. You need to learn a programming language that runs on all key operating systems such as Linux, Mac OS X, and Microsoft windows, and one that is more reliable (does not contain pointers, which is case with other languages based on C). You need to learn Python.

Python will provide you all that, and since new platforms like Raspberry Pi are Python based, learning Python will place you at an ideal place where you can enjoy the internet of things of opportunities and anyway (in case you have not yet noticed), Python's popularity for the internet of things is really growing.

That is just a tip of the iceberg, with Python, opportunities and possibilities are simply endless.

This book will introduce you to the Python programming language and make sure that after reading the guide, you shall be aware of the basics of the language and able to create simple Python programs. This book the first in a series of 3 books meant to help you learn Python programming, from beginner to intermediate then advanced level. As such, this book will handle everything you need to build a strong understanding of the basics of Python programming language.

Thanks again for downloading this book. I hope you enjoy it!

To make this book easy to understand, we will start by building a basic understanding of what Python really is, how it came into being and such information before we getting to the detailed explanations of how the programing language works and how to use it.

Understanding Python: A Detailed Background

It is important to build up to the events that preceded the creation of python, the programming language before we even define it.

Guido Van Rossum Created Python In 1989

Rossum used to work at Centrum Voor Wiskunde en Informatica (CWI) in the early 1980s. His job was implementing the programming language known as ABC. During the later 1980s—while still at CWI—he began searching for a scripting language that had syntax similar to ABC but one that had access to the system calls of Amoeba (during this time, Rossum was working on Amoeba, a freshly distributed operating system). After looking and finding nothing that could suit his needs, Rossum decided to design a simple scripting language that could overcome ABC's inadequacies.

In the late 1980s, Rossum began developing the new script and in 1991, launched the opening version of the programming language. This first release had a Modula-3 module system. This language was later on named "Python."

Why the Name "Python?"

Many people usually think that name 'Python' comes from a snake because the Python's logo shows an image of a blue and yellow snake. Nonetheless, the real story behind the naming is a bit different.

In the 1970s, BBC had a popular TV show that van Rossum was a big fan of; the show was Monty Python's Fly Circus. Thus, when Rossum developed the language, he, for some reason only known to him, decided to name the project 'Python'.

The Timeline: Tracing the Release of Different Versions of Python

Python 1.0, the first ever Python version, was introduced in 1991. Since Python came into being, and its first version introduced, the language has evolved and reached up to version 3.x.

Please check out the summary chart below that illustrates the timeline of the various Python programming language versions.

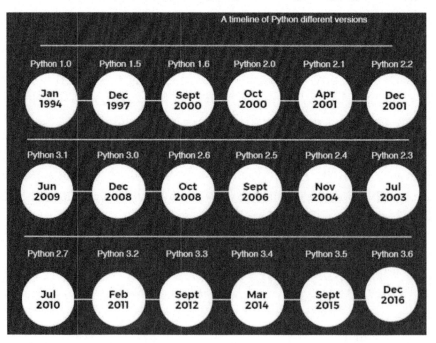

Each of the versions indicated above contains a number of series; for instance, python 3.6 released in 2016 is currently at 3.6. 4 as at 2017-12-19.

Now that you have a bit of understanding of how Python became what it is today, let's get a bit technical whereby we will define what Python (the programming language) really is.

Python Defined

Fair warning: What you are about to read will sound a bit technical. Please refer to the glossary for meanings of certain terms.

Python is a high level programming language (a language made to be simple for humans to write and read) that is also object-oriented (organized around or based on objects instead of actions or data instead of logic).

Compared to other programming languages, Python is very simple and easy to learn because it requires a very unique syntax that emphasizes readability. As a developer, you can read and translate the Python code a lot easier than is the case with other languages. This readability reduces the overall cost of program maintenance and development since it allows you to work with teams collaboratively without any significant experience or language barriers.

You should note that Python has speed as a core functionality, and therefore, it works perfectly well with applications such as photo development. In fact, you will find Python embedded in important programs such as Paint Shop Pro and GIMP and is the favored Google developers' language—used on YouTube!

Actually, the YouTube architect Cuong Do has spoken broadly on the efficiency of the Python and the 'record speed' the language has allowed them to work with. I could thus say that Python is among the fastest programming languages you could ever incorporate in development particularly when speed is your primary factor.

Besides that, impressed by its number of libraries, the University of Maryland has opted to use Python to aid the development of their courses. If you are a video game designer, you could benefit from the extensive set of libraries within Python that are important resources given a 'Py' in the name for identification purposes.

Python also finds use in adaptive technology (the tools or technology designed to offer enhancements or alternative ways of interacting with technology—this helps disabled people perform certain tasks) and in this regard, it has contributed to movements such as "one laptop per child."

You can compare Python to other dynamic languages such as PHP, PERL, and Java. When you do so, you will realize that Python is simpler and more consistent—and many Python enthusiasts or folks who have had a good experience with the language will attest to that.

For instance, consider that Python uses key words while other languages still use punctuation marks. The fact that Python uses key words makes things easier especially for beginners and because of it, the learning process is cumulatively shorter and fun. We will learn more about that in the subsequent chapters when we begin learning and writing Python code examples.

Right now though, let us see how python really works. We will try to understand that by briefly looking at how programming languages have been evolving over time.

How Python Works

To understand how Python works today, we have to take a few steps back in time.

Machine code (the first generation Computer languages)

In machine code, a computer processor can perform only a certain number of commands that are very simple and kept in a sequence of bits or numbers. Usually, programmers use a hexadecimal system to write these instructions so that their reading is not so much of a chore.

Nonetheless, with the instructions so limited, all you can do here is recapitulate addresses and skip between instructions. You might already know that in the world of programming, you do not just add two numbers; rather, what you do is look at the addresses of the numbers in memory and then recapitulate or sum them using a number of different instructions.

Just to give you perspective, look at the example below that shows what the addition of two numbers would appear in the hex

```
2104
1105
3106
7001
0053
FFFE
0000
```

The instructions go to the processor in binary. You will notice that this kind of code is very unreadable and depends on the instruction set of the CPU in question. You can rest assured that programming in this language is extremely galling but unfortunately, all programs have to be compiled in binary format for execution by a computer processor.

Machine code   Processor

The assembler (second-generation computer languages)

While the ASM or assembler boasts of being human-readable, it is not any simpler than machine code. The instructions here contain readable (to a human) text codes that eliminate the need for human memorization of each one of the combinations of numbers. The instruction codes are afterwards compiled into binary code. When you add two numbers in the assembler, you should expect something similar to this:

```
ORG 100
LDA
ADD B
STA C
HLT
DEC 83
DEC -2
DEC 0
END
```

As I mentioned, this one is a bit more readable to a human; however, most programmers do not have a clue how the program really works.

The third generation programming languages

These ones have a better amount of abstraction about how the computer sees the program. Instead of forcing you to adapt to the way the computer thinks—which is arcane—the language focuses more on the way you see the program.

At the introduction of these languages, the numbers started being perceived as variables and the code would contain some sort of 'mathematical notation' kind of aesthetic.

When you, for instance, add two numbers in the C language, it will pretty much go like so:

```
int main (void)
{
    int a, b, c;
    a = 83;
    b = -2;
    c = a + b;
    return 0;
}
```

Anyone can assume the workings of this by merely looking at it. As you can see, it sums up the 83 and -2, and then stores the product in a variable called C. Third generation languages have one obvious advantage: they have very high readability compared to all the other previous languages.

A recap

If we are still together, let us do a recap:

From the name 'high level language' (whose meaning you know already), you might deduce that there are 'low-level languages' as well—at times called machine languages or the other category known as assembly languages.

Machine language is simply the encoding of program instructions in binary such that the computer can directly execute them. The assembly language uses a format that is a bit easier to refer to the low-level instructions. Therefore, high-level language programs—including the ones in assembly language—need processing before they run. This additional processing takes a bit of time, which is a little disadvantage of the high-level languages. Nonetheless, the high-level languages have numerous advantages.

First, it is a lot easier to program in high-level languages. The programs written in a high-level language typically take a lot less time to write; they are also shorter, generally easier to read, and are relatively more likely to be correct. Secondly, they are portable. This means you can run them on different types of computers with few or minimal modifications. Conversely, a low-level program has to run on one kind of computer before modifying or rewriting it to make sure it runs on another.

Therefore, you will find that nearly all programs in existence today use high-level languages. Only a few specialized applications use low-level languages.

Let us continue.

Object-oriented programming came into the picture as time passed and as the demand for code optimization increased. I will talk more about this later. The third generation languages fall into two categories:

Compiled languages

Also called unmanaged languages, compiled languages typically have their source code written in a language humans can fully understand. For the processor to execute the source code, it needs to be translated into machine code though. A compiler completes this process. The compiler compiles the whole program into the machine code.

Source code   Compiler   Machine code   Processor

Put differently, a compiler simply reads the program and translates it before it (the program) begins running. The high-level program is thus referred to as the source code while the program that is translated is known as the executable or object code. When the program is compiled, it can be executed multiple times without the need for any further translation.

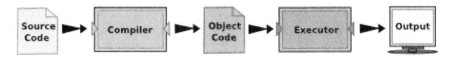

Here is a brief overview of some of the advantages of compiled languages.

1. They are fast: It is only in the course of one-time compilation that the program slows down. When a program is compiled, it runs just as fast as a program written in ASM or even faster owing to compiler optimizations.

2. There is inaccessibility of source code. Modifying a program distributed in compiled form is difficult if you lack the source code.

3. It provides ease of detecting errors in the source code. If there happens to be an error in the source code, the whole process of compilation crashes and you, the programmer, automatically gets to see where you messed up. You can imagine how much this simplifies the development of software.

The disadvantages include the following:

1. The program has a platform dependency, that is, on the operating system or the processor. You cannot take a pre-compiled program and then run it on a different platform without tweaking or recompiling it somehow.

2. You cannot edit it. After the compilation of a program into machine code, there is no other way of editing it; re-compiling is the only way.

3. Issues of memory management. Computers execute instructions mechanically; this makes it likely to run into sporadic errors related to memory overflows. The compiled languages do not come with automatic memory management features and thus, they tend to be more of a hassle in this respect. The main cause of run-time errors is manual memory management the compilation cannot detect. Pascal, C language and C++, its successor, are examples of compiled languages.

Interpreted languages

Python belongs to this category of programming languages. Interpreted languages aim to solve issues regarding portability and in many other respects, try to make the lives of programmers somewhat easier. Most modern programming languages are interpreted languages.

Interpreters work a lot like compilers but rather than translating the whole program all at the same time, they only translate what is required at a particular moment in time.

The name 'interpreter' simply comes from the profession we all know of, interpretation, where the interpreter is the person who acts as an intermediary for people who do not understand each other's languages. The interpreter listens and translates what each party is saying to a language they understand and the conducts the translation as each one of them speaks.

The interpreted languages operate the same way. The interpreter reads the source code line after line before compiling it into machine code, executing it, and then throwing it away.

While interpretation is not a quick way to run programs, it has a number of significant advantages. To improve speed, it is possible to cache results. In addition, today, the quality and readability of code has proved more important than performance. The reason for this is that our computers are very fast but as applications become a lot more complex by the day, it becomes increasingly easier to create errors particularly when using the older languages.

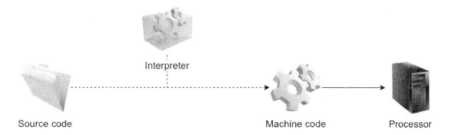

Source code   Machine code   Processor

Put differently, an interpreter is responsible for reading a high level program after which it executes it. In simpler terms, the interpreter does pretty much what the program commands. It processes the program bit by bit, reading lines alternately and conducting computations.

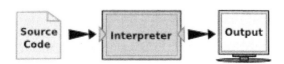

NOTE: Many programming languages in existence today, including Python, use both processes whereby the first thing that happens in the compilation of the source code into a lower-level language known as byte code and then interpretation by a program known as virtual machine. In the case of Python, programmers interact with the language, which is why Python is an interpreted language.

The usage

There are two ways you can use the Python interpreter: as the program mode and shell mode. In the shell mode, you simply type the Python expressions into the shell and the interpreter shows the result immediately.

Take a look at the example below that illustrates the Python shell at work.

```
$ python3
Python 3.2 (r32:88445, Mar 25 2011, 19:28:28)
[GCC 4.5.2] on linux2
Type "help", "copyright", "credits" or "license" for more
information.
>>> 2 + 3
5
>>>
```

These signs '>>>' are known as the Python prompt. The interpreter shows that it is ready for instructions by using the prompt. When 2+3 was typed, the interpreter evaluated the expression and in turn replied 5. On the following line, it gave a new prompt to show that it is ready for additional input.

When you work in the interpreter directly, you experience convenience for testing short parts of code since you get immediate feedback. You can think of it as a kind of scratch paper you can use to work out problems.

As an alternative, you can also write a whole program by placing Python instruction lines in a file and then use the interpreter to execute the file contents in entirety. This file is what we usually call a source code. For instance, you can use a text editor to create a source code file called firstprogram.py that contains the following:

```
print("My first program adds two numbers, 2 and 3:")
print(2 + 3)
```

Conventionally, files containing Python programs contain names ending with .py. This convention helps your operating system and other programs recognize a file as having python code.

```
$ python firstprogram.py
My first program adds two numbers, 2 and 3:
5
```

Advantages of Interpretation

Before we continue, here is a brief overview of some of the advantages of interpretation:

1. The programs are portable. If the platform has an interpreter, your program will run on the said platform—it is a lot simpler to develop an interpreter than a compiler.

2. Simplicity in development: Today, there is no need to deal with manual memory management because something called 'garbage collector' can do that for you. In Python and other languages, you do not really have to specify the data

types, something that leads to more comfortable data structures—you will notice this as you advance in the book.

3. Stability: The interpreter really understands code and owing to this fact, it can find errors that the compiled programs would ultimately execute. Interpreting programs is safer and better than compiling them. Further, using this language type brings reflection into play—in reflection, a program can examine itself in the course of the run-time.

4. Ease of editing: You can write programs in sections and then upload them to the targeted destination any time you wish since the code does not need explicit compilation. In other words, you can easily edit it on the fly.

The adding program's source code in python would appear something like this:

```
a = 83
b = -2
c = a + b
print(c)
```

You need to notice that we only have the core algorithm and no other syntax; you do not even have to specify the variable types-guess things are too simple here!

Disadvantages of Interpretation

Well, we cannot lack a few disadvantages with interpreters:

1. There are still speed issues. At times, interpretation can be very slow and because of this, you will not use your computer's capacity to the fullest. This, however, has various workarounds.

2. There are still difficulties in spotting errors. With interpretation, compilation happens during run time; this makes it impossible for errors to pop up before execution of the code. This can be annoying at times. Nonetheless, you will still err less than you would otherwise do in the compiled languages.

3. Vulnerability: Since the program is distributed as a source code and thus, any person can change or even steal some parts of it, issues of vulnerability crop up.

With the information above, you should be able to look at Python as a modern programming language that, even though not the fastest, the source code is shorter and has fewer errors than the compiled languages of the older versions.

At this point, I believe it would be great to have a glossary to explain different terms that you will find often in the book.

Python Glossary

This section is going to be relatively short; it will simply define the terms you can expect to find used in forums dedicated to Python and within the language itself. As we head further into the book, you will learn more about these terms:

Instruction sets: These are the sets of the entire instructions contained in machine code that a central processing unit can recognize and execute.

Binary: Binary is a set of files created once you compile the object code that runs on machines.

Run time: Also called execution time, run time refers to the time a program is running or executing.

Shell: Shell is the programming layer that understands and executes commands you enter as a user.

Pip: Pip refers to the package management system used for the installation and management of software packages written in Python.

IDLE (Integrated Development Environment): IDLE refers to Python's integrated development environment bundled with the language's default implementation.

Char: Char refers to the characters generally in programming languages

Delimeter: This is the sequence of a single or more characters used to specify the boundary between independent and separate regions in data streams such as plain text.

Arguments: Arguments are variables or independent items containing codes or data.

26

Assignment: In programming, an assignment is a statement used to set into a variable name a value.

Iteration: Iteration refers to a process where instructions or structures are recurred sequentially in a given number of times, or until some condition is met.

Hashing: This refers to the change of a string or characters into a typically shorter value with a fixed length or key representing the initial string.

Immutable object: This is an object that has a state that become impossible to modify once created.

Zero or Zero value: This refers to the unique and known quantity the zero value that is significant in mathematics.

Null value: Refers to a non-value; it acts as some sort of placeholder for an unknown or unspecified data value

Modular design: A modular design is a design approach that divides a system into little sections known as skids or modules; you can create modules independently and then use them in various systems.

Docstring: This is a string literal occurring as the first function statement, module, method definition, or class.

Objects: Objects are those things you first think about when you are designing a program; they are the units of code ultimately derived from the process.

Class: Class is a sort of distinct mini-program that has its own peculiar context—that is the properties or variables and functions or methods.

Keep these terms and definitions in mind because as we delve deeper into the world of Python programming, they will appear at many areas.

With the glossary in mind, you shouldn't have any problem reading the book since you can refer to this content whenever you see something you don't understand. Let's now start using Python.

How to Download and Install Python

In this section, we will discuss how to download and install Python on Windows and Ubuntu platforms (to act as examples). As I mentioned earlier, you can install Python on almost all the operating systems we have today and therefore, this tutorial is just a general blueprint of how to undertake the process.

The first thing we shall do is talk about the difference in the two major versions just to elucidate the issue of what version is ideal or suitable.

First Things First: Which Version Is Suitable: 2.X Or 3.X?

As a beginner Python programmer, one of the things that might confuse you is the different versions of the language that are currently available. Even though Python 3 is the most current generation of Python, you will note that many programmers still use Python 2.x.

Even today, you will not really find a straightforward answer to the question of the Python version you should use as the decision will depend on what you want to accomplish. Python 3 is indeed the future of the language but some programmers opt to go with python 2.x because some older libraries and packages only work in Python 2.

Why there are Different Versions of the Language

Programming languages are always evolving as developers

continue extending the language's functionality and ironing out the quirks known to cause concerns for developers.

First introduced in 2008, Python 3 sought to make Python easier to use and change the way it deals with strings to correspond with the current demands placed on the language. The programmers accustomed to the program in Python 2 at times find it hard to adjust to the fresh challenges, but the tenderfoots usually find the current versions of the language more logical.

Python 3.x is different from earlier Python releases primarily because it is the first ever Python release that is incompatible with the earlier versions. Programmers do not usually need to worry about minor updates—such as from 2.6 to 2.7 because the only thing they usually do is alter the internal workings of the language and do not need the programmers to alter their syntax.

There is a much more significant change between Python 2.7.x and Python 3.x as the code that worked in the former may require rewriting in a different way so that it works in Python 3.x

Downloading and installing Python 3.6.4 on Windows (32 bit)

At the time of writing this book, the latest version of Python is 3.6 (and 3.6.4 series). We are going to discuss how to download and install Python 3.6.4 for the 32-bit version of the language (64-bit in the next section). Installing the program will automatically install IDLE, the documentation, and pip as well—and create file associations and shortcuts. This will eliminate the need to set up the environment variables once the installation completes.

Before you begin, ensure you do not have Python installed on your computer already. You can do this by opening the command prompt and typing 'python' on it. If you do not have the program installed on your computer, you will see something similar to the image below.

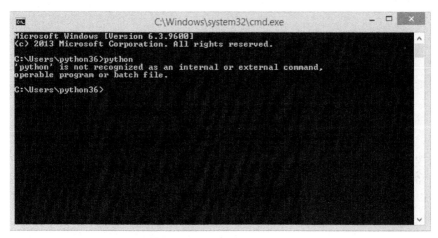

You can download the Python setup file by visiting Python's official website and under downloads in the menu bar, clicking on the latest version of Python (3.6.4 in this case).

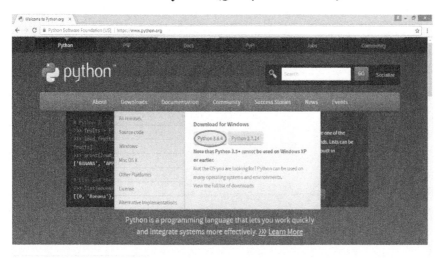

Alternatively, you can click on the link below to download the setup file:

https://www.python.org/ftp/python/3.6.4/python-3.6.4.exe

Once the file has downloaded, find the setup file in 'downloads' that has the name 'pythin-3.6.4.exe'. Run it and wait for something like this:

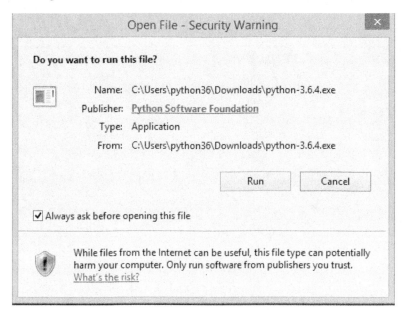

When you click on Run, you will see something like:

The option 'add python 3.6 to PATH' is by default left unchecked: make sure to check it. Now click 'install now'. The window resembling the image below will appear if the setup is successful.

Let us now check whether python 3.6 has installed successfully. Simply open the command prompt and then type 'python' in it. You will have to close and reopen the prompt if you had not closed it from earlier. You should see something that looks like:

You will need to check that the interpreter is functioning properly through the prompt:

```
C:\Windows\system32\cmd.exe - python
Microsoft Windows [Version 6.3.9600]
(c) 2013 Microsoft Corporation. All rights reserved.

C:\Users\python36>python
Python 3.6.4 (v3.6.4:d48eceb, Dec 19 2017, 06:04:45) [MSC v.1900 32 bit (Intel)]
on win32
Type "help", "copyright", "credits" or "license" for more information.
>>> print("python programming tutorials")
python programming tutorials
>>>
```

You also have the choice of searching IDLE and running python commands through it.

```
Python 3.6.4 Shell
File  Edit  Shell  Debug  Options  Window  Help
Python 3.6.4 (v3.6.4:d48eceb, Dec 19 2017, 06:04:45) [MSC v.1900 32 bit (Intel)]
on win32
Type "copyright", "credits" or "license()" for more information.
>>> print("python programming tutorials")
python programming tutorials
>>>
```

Installation of the 64-Bit Version

To install the 64-bit version, simply go to the official website and go to the menu bar. Click on downloads and then windows, and wait to see something like this:

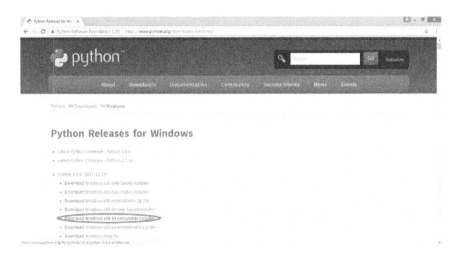

Now click on the highlighted area 'download windows x84-64 executable installer.'

Alternatively, you download the setup file from this link.

When the download completes, search for the setup file named 'python- 3.6.4- amd64.exe' from the 'downloads' folder.

Now run it. Everything from here should be straightforward and the installation steps are the same as the ones discussed in the section above.

Installing Python on Ubuntu and Linux Mint

The process here is just as simple as the one we have just discussed. Just follow the steps below.

1: Install the needed packages

First, you need to install the Python prerequisites before moving on to the next steps using the command below:

```
sudo apt-get install build-essential checkinstall
```

```
sudo apt-get install libreadline-gplv2-dev libncursesw5-dev
libssl-dev libsqlite3-dev tk-dev libgdbm-dev libc6-dev libbz2-dev
```

2: Download Python 3.6.4

You can download the program from the official site (just as we discussed in the previous sections) of Python or download the latest version as follows:

```
cd /usr/src
```

```
sudo wget https://www.python.org/ftp/python/3.6.4/Python-
3.6.4.tgz
```

You can now extract the downloaded package as follows:

```
sudo tar xzf Python-3.6.4.tgz
```

3: Now compile the Python source

Use the set of commands below to compile the source code of the program on your computer. You can use the option '— enable-optimizations' with the configure command to enable extra supports such as bz2 support, SSL. The command 'make altinstall' will not overwrite the existing installation.

```
cd Python-3.6.4
sudo ./configure --enable-optimizations
sudo make altinstall
```

4: Check the version

At this point, you have successfully installed Python 3.6 on your computer. You need to check the Python version installed with the command below:

python3.6 -V

Python 3.6.4

This resource describes how to install Python on Mac OS X.

With Python successfully installed, we can now begin interacting with it.

Python Programming 101: Interacting With Python in Different Ways

Now that you have installed Python on your computer, let us start interacting with it:

Know the Consoles

After installing Python, the first thing you want to know how is how to interact with it flawlessly. In this regard, you will realize that there are numerous ways to achieve that. The first way you can learn is interacting with the program's interpreter using the console of your operating system.

A console (also called a command prompt or terminal) is a way of interacting with your operating system using texts—just like interacting with your desktop using your mouse is the method of interacting with your system graphically.

Let us see how you can open a console on the various operating systems:

Opening a Console on Mac OS X

Terminal is the name given to the standard console program in Mac OS X. To open the terminal, simply go to applications, then click on utilities and then double click on the terminal program. Alternatively, you can search for it in the system using the system search tool located at the top right.

You will interact with your computer using the command line

terminal; a window will pop up with message that looks something like this:

```
mycomputer:~ myusername$
```

Opening a console on Linux OS

We have different distributions of the Linux operating system such as Mint, Fedora, and Ubuntu. Thus, these distributions may have different console programs commonly called a terminal. The particular terminal you start up, as well as how you do it depends on the distribution you are using. Take Ubuntu for instance; here, you will likely have to open Gnome terminal that presents a prompt that looks something like this:

```
myusername@mycomputer:~$
```

Opening the Console on Windows OS

In windows OS, the console is the prompt named 'cmd'. The shortest way to start the cmd is using the following key combination:

```
Windows log button+R
```

Pressing that will pop up a run dialog where you will then have to type cmd and click on enter or okay. Alternatively, you can search for it at the search menu and wait to get something like this:

```
C:\Users\myusername>
```

NOTE: The command prompt in windows has limited capabilities and is not as very powerful as in the other operating systems such as OS X and Linux. Therefore, you might want to start the Python interpreter directly or use Python's IDLE program that comes with it. You will find these options in your start menu. We will talk about using the IDLE in more detail in a moment.

The Windows PowerShell

The Windows PowerShell is a CLI (command-line interface) for the windows OS. A command line interface is a kind of program we use to tell the computer what to do using textual commands. Well, technically, the PowerShell is more than just the CLI; it enables you to automate tasks and perform multiple things with a single command.

Getting started with PowerShell is quite simple. All you have to do is search for PowerShell on your computer. You may find that you have a number of different options such as PowerShell (x86) and PowerShell ISE.

The Integrated Scripting Environment or ISE is a handy tool that equips you with the ability to write scripts as you go and that has an expedient look-up for the entire group of PowerShell commands. At this point in your Python programming journey, this might be more than you would need.

The 'x86' on the other hand is here for backwards compatibility—if you have been around computers for a while, you will remember the old Intel processors known as 286, 836 and so on from the 80s and 90s. That is exactly what the 'x86' is getting at; and it is a 32-bit version.

To use this program, you want a 64-bit, and so you can use the one just with the name 'windows PowerShell'. When you open it, it should look something like this:

In case you do not fancy the white on blue, simply right click the top bar, select 'properties' and then 'colors' to change things. You may have to close and open PowerShell again so that it displays properly.

How to navigate

The good thing about PowerShell is that it always lets you know where you are because it gives you that information in the prompt. In our case here, we see the following:

C:\Users\Ted>

You should be able to see something similar to this only with your username. In case you do not, you can type the following:

sl ~

Just ensure to put the space–that will take you to your home directory that is:

C:\Users\YOURUSERNAME.

Here, your account's name (on the directory of the machine) replaces the word 'YOURUSERNAME'. Directory is a word that represents 'folder', and PowerShell considers your user folder and not the desktop to be your home. You should note that your desktop is only another folder inside your user folder—you can imagine it as a subdirectory of the user directory. When you

41

enter sl~, it's like you've opened the folder known as 'users' and then YOURUSERNAME with your GUI.

As we move forward, you will gain better understanding of PowerShell and its usage with Python.

The First Steps in Python with IDLE

As we begin, here are some conventions of formatting to guide you:

Output statements and python commands are usually set in **bold** like in **print "Hello World!"**

Secondly, the code blocks are shaded in grey boxes and the code written in these boxes contains colored highlighting for various parts of the Python language such as comments, variables, and commands and so on.

Know how to start IDLE

IDLE (Integrated Development Environment) for Python is a software package you can run the Python program with–it lets you test the Python commands, edit, and run the Python programs.

In a typical IDLE session, you will interactively try Python commands, and then run and edit the python programs. In these activities, you will start an IDLE session and run a few simple scripts.

NOTE: I do not recommend opening Python files that end with the extension '.py' by double clicking them; instead, open the scripts form within the IDLE session using *File>>* Open. The reason behind this is the behavior you get can be unexpected even though it will not cause any harm.

Let us continue:

If you are using the windows operating system, you will start IDLE from the Python XY package. Open IDLE from the start menu as follows:

Start~ All programs~ Python 3.6.4~IDLE

You will get a window named 'Python Shell' that looks something like this:

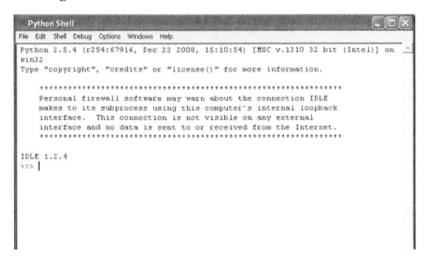

If you are using Mac OS X, you can open IDLE from the applications folder in the following steps:

Applications ~ Python ~IDLE

A 'python shell' will then pop up–it will look something like:

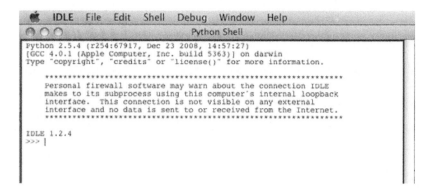

Let us now start running some scripts so that you know how to run them; you can find these scripts in the examples folder which you can download as a zip file <u>here</u>.

Download the folder, unzip it, and check the list of examples in it.

Go back to the IDLE program and then to the examples folder by using *File ~ Open* in the Windows OS or Mac OS. Open the file labeled 'bounce' that may appear as bounce.py or bounce in the directory catalogue.

Choose *Run ~ Run Module* in the menu (you can use F5 as a shortcut for this). This should produce an animated bouncing ball as shown below:

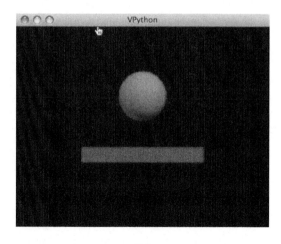

What you are looking at is the scene from a virtual camera's perspective—you can use your mouse to move the camera around the scene. You can zoom, pan, or even rotate the camera to various orientations. The mouse controls are not the same on Mac and windows systems.

You can hold down the right mouse button and then move it to rotate the camera. On Mac systems, press the command before moving the mouse. Try rotating the camera now.

You typically hold the middle button down and then move the mouse to pan and zoom. If you are using a Mac system, just hold the right and left buttons or simply press the option key before moving the mouse. You can now try to pan and zoom.

Are you ready to move on to the next example? If so, close the window that has the animation. The subsequent example plots some data. In the folder labeled examples, look for the file named 'matplotlib_example.py', which may appear as 'matplotlib_example.py' or 'matplotlib_example'.

Choose Run Module – you can also use F5 as the shortcut (before anything happens, you might have to wait for a minute or two). When you do this though, the earth's surface global mean temperature plot should appear- this is as a function of year for a number of decades as indicated below. The plot gets its data from the NASA GISS website.

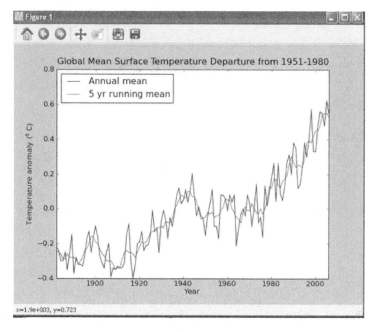

You can now open and run any of the scripts in the examples folder freely—for instance, stars.py, and gas.py. Moreover, you can edit them, save them, and run them to change them; note that IDLE only runs scripts saved to the disk.

To learn more, you can begin tinkering with the scripts—it does not matter whether you understand only a part of what is happening in the scripts as you can have fun changing them and checking the result.

When done, you can quit IDLE, and continue with the next part.

A recap

Let us have a little recap to make sure we are still together:

The most basic means to create and run a python program is creating an empty file that has the .py extension, and pointing to the same file from the command line using 'python filename.py.'As an alternative, you can work with the default Python IDLE that comes installed with Python. You can then be able to write your code and execute it within IDLE.

Nonetheless, if you want to be even more productive, you can try something else that is different from the first two options; try using something like the atom editor.

Using the Atom editor

Atom is an open source free text editor, which means it provides all the code for you to read and adjust for your personal use and maybe even your own contribution to improvements.

The Atom editor is a creation of GitHub. Its popularity has grown from the slogan "the hackable text editor for the 21st century." The program is very flexible and has good support for external packages; this makes it a very powerful Interactive Development Environment (IDE). It is very customizable and hence the allusion 'the hackable text editor.'

The following steps describe how you can get and use this program.

Download and install it

Go to this website to download it and install it. When you install the program, open the command line and type 'atom'. You can also ensure atom is already been added to your search environment or path variables in case that does not work.

You should expect something like this:

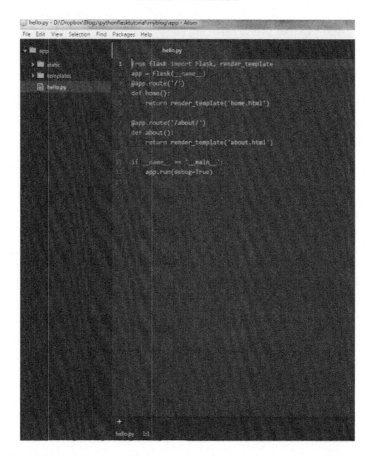

You should also note that there is a more convenient way of opening Atom: by clicking on a folder where your files are and then going to 'open with Atom'. This action will simply add all the folder's files to the tree view —as the screenshot above clearly shows. This is excellent when the web app or program you are developing has multiple files. This means you can simply jump from one file to another and edit them from inside Atom.

Executing a python file in Atom

One way of executing a python file in Atom is opening the command line and pointing to the file paths; you can also use an important atom package called platform-ide-terminal. This package integrates with Atom so that you can execute files from Atom.

For the installation of the package, go to 'file' and then 'settings'. When you install the 'terminal-plus' package, you can get the tool and go to the packages to open a terminal instance. You can also open a terminal in a faster way by clicking on the plus sign added at the foot of the atom window.

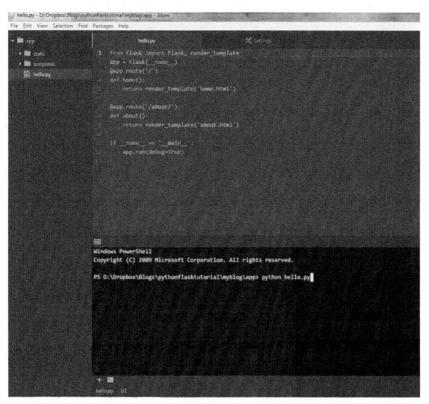

You can see the terminal points to your files' main directory. From there, you can now execute the python scripts as the screenshot above shows.

NOTE: You can divide the editor into multiple windows. When you have more than one file opened within Atom, go to view and then panes and click on split right. This will send your current file to the right half of the window–this will improve your productivity when you are dealing with separate files.

The next step is to write something with Python. We will use the atom text editor so that you understand more how to use the program.

How to Write Your First Python Program

Type the text below into one file called ex1.py. Python operates best with files that end in .py. On all platforms, the atom text editor should appear like the image below:

You should not mind so much if your editor does not look the same as the screenshot above- it should only be a bit close at the least. You may see a different header on your window-- perhaps a bit different window header and different colors. In addition, the left side of the window will not have the name 'zedshaw' but will show the directory you used to save your files. Such differences are all okay.

When creating the file, keep the following points in mind:

1. In the example above, I did not personally type the numbers on the left side. You don't key in the line numbers into the scripts; these numbers are in the book so that I can mention

the particular lines by saying- "look at the fifth line", "or line 5".

2. The print that is there at the beginning of the line ought to be there and looks much the same as what I already have ex1.py. For it to work, every character needs to match. The color does not really matter; the only thing that matters is the characters that you actually type.

Type the following in the terminal to run the file.

python ex1.py

If you did everything properly, then you should be able to see an output similar to mine as shown in the images below. If you have something different, it simply means you have done something wrong (and no, your computer is not the problem).

You should see the following on:

Mac OS X terminal

```
zedshaw$ python ex1.py
Hello World!
Hello Again
I like typing this.
This is fun.
Yay! Printing.
I'd much rather you 'not'.
I "said" do not touch this.
zedshaw$
```

Windows (in powershell):

You might start seeing quite a number of different names before the command 'python ex1.py', but the most important part is typing the command and seeing an output similar to what we have here.

If there is an error, it will appear as follows:

```
$ python ex/ex1.py
  File "ex/ex1.py", line 3
    print "I like typing this.
                              ^
```

SyntaxError: EOL while scanning string literal

It is essential that you be able to read the error messages since you will be making many of them. Everyone makes these kinds of mistakes. Let us look at the error line by line.

In the terminal, you ran your command to run the ex1.py script.

Python inform us that there is an error in the file ex.1py specifically on line 3.

This line of code is "printed" for you to see it.

It then includes a caret character (^) to point at the problem. You can notice the missing double-quote character (") can't you?

Lastly, we have a printed SyntaxError that says something about the possible error. Typically, these are quite cryptic but if you copy the text and paste it into a search engine, you will probably find someone else who has had a similar error and maybe a way of fixing it as well.

The "Adding Two Numbers" Program

If you have been looking around, you should have noticed that the "Hello World" program is the one commonly used to introduce a programming language such as Python to beginners.

"Hello, World!" is a simple program that produces 'Hello, world!' as the output. Python is one of the simplest languages not only to learn but also to use to create the 'Hello, World!' program which is as simple as just having the inscription print("Hello, World!"). We are thus going to have a different program. This is a program of writing two numbers.

```python
# Add two numbers
num1 = 3
num2 = 5
sum = num1+num2
print(sum)
```

Let us examine how this program works...

In line 1, we have # Add two numbers. Any line that starts with the symbol '#' is a comment. In programming, comments define the purpose of a code and serve to help you, the programmer, understand code's intent. Compilers and interpreters usually ignore the comments.

In line 2, we have num1=3. In this case, num1 is a variable. You can store a value in a variable and thus, 3 here is stored in this variable.

In line 3, we have num5 =3. Likewise, num2 is a variable and 5 is the value stored in it.

In line 4, we have sum=num1 + num2. Both variables, num1 and num2, are combined by the operator '+'. The result of the addition is then stored in another variable known as 'sum'.

In line 5, we have print(sum). The function 'print()' simply prints the output or product on the screen. In the case here, 8 is the output printed on the screen.

More on variables is next up.

Important Points to Remember

To represent a statement in the Python program, we use newline or enter. It is not mandatory to use the semicolon at the end of the statement—which is not the case in languages such as JavaScript, C or C++, and PHP.

Python actually recommends that you ignore the semicolon right at the end of the statement. Instead of using {} -curly braces, you can use indentations in representation of a block.

```
im_a_parent:
im_a_child:
   im_a_grand_child
im_another_child:

   im_another_grand_child
```

We shall now talk a bit more about variable and a few other things you should know:

Variables, Strings, Lists, Tuples, Dictionaries

Let us start with variables:

Variables

As we saw earlier, a variable stores a value. To clarify the concept further, let us look at a few more examples:

```
message = "Hello Python world!"

print(message)
```

You can change a variable's value at any point you want.

```
message = "Hello Python world!"
print(message)

message = "Python is my favorite language!"

print(message)
```

The Naming Rules

Variables can only have letters, underscores, and numbers. The names of the variables can begin with an underscore or a letter, never with a number.

When writing variable names, you should not include spaces. Instead, you can use underscores. For instance, you can use 'my_name' instead of 'my name.'

You cannot substitute variable names for python keywords. Python keywords are special words that form Python's vocabulary. A Python keyword is a kind of reserved word that you cannot use as an identifier. The list below contains the keywords for Python language:

False	def	if	raise
None	del	import	return
True	elif	in	try
and	else	is	while
as	except	lambda	with
assert	finally	nonlocal	yield
break	for	not	
class	from	or	
continue	global	pass	

Names of variables ought to be descriptive but not too long. For instance, bs_wheels is better than simply 'wheels' or total_number_of_wheels_on_a_bus.

You have to be careful about using the uppercase letter O and the lowercase letter I in areas where someone might confuse them with the numbers 0 and 1.

The Name Error

When you are using variables, you will come across a common error at one point or another. Check out the code below to see if you can work out why it brings about an error:

```
message = "Thank you for sharing Python with the world, Guido!"

print(mesage)
```

Let us now look through the error message. First, you see it as a NameError and then you see the file that brought about the error, and a green arrow displays the line in the file that caused the error. You then get a more specific response that the "name 'message' isn't defined."

You already may have found the error source. You spelled the message in two ways that are different. The python program does not really care whether you use the variable name 'message' or 'message'. It only cares that your variable's spellings match each time you use them.

This is very important because it ensure you have a variable 'name' that has one name in it, then another variable 'names' containing some names in it.

You can fix the NameErrors by ensuring all your variable names have consistent spelling.

```
message = "Thank you for sharing Python with the world, Guido!"

print(message)
```

Strings

Strings are bits of texts you want to 'export' out of the program you are writing or display to someone. The python program knows that you intend to have something as a string when you place 'single quotes' or 'double quotes' around your text.

Python has an in built string class (we will talk about classes in a bit) named 'str'. This string class has numerous important features (we have an earlier module known a 'string' that you should not use).

The string literals can be bounded using single quotes or double quotes–single quotes are the most popularly used. Backlash escapes usually work pretty much the standard way inside both double and single quoted literals such as in \n\'\. " You can as well include single quotes in double quoted string literal. For instance, "I didn't do it" and similarly, the single quoted string cab have double quotes.

String literals can even span several lines but at the end of every line, there has to be a backlash \ to escape the newline. Again, the string literals within triple quotes like these"""" or"" can span many lines of text.

Python strings are also immutable. This means once created, they are unchangeable. This immutable style is also present in Java strings. Since Java strings are unchangeable, we create new strings on the fly to stand for computed values. For instance, the 'hello' + 'there' expression takes in both strings 'hello' and 'there' and creates a new string 'hellothere'.

String characters can also accessible using the standard syntax '[]'; just like C++ and Java, Python uses sort of zero-based indexing; thus, if str is 'hello' str [1] is 'e'. In this case, Python can also raise an error if the index is off limits for the string. Unlike Perl, the Python style is to stop if it cannot clearly tell what to do instead of structuring a default value. The handy syntax you can see below works to derive any substring from a string. The function len(string) returns the length of a string. The syntax [] and the function len() work on any type of sequence- lists, strings and so on. Python tries making its operations work through different types.

NOTE: To avoid blocking out the function 'len()' do not use 'len' as the name for the variable.

The operator '+'can concatenate or join two strings. As you would notice in the code below, the variables are not exactly pre-declared—you only need to assign to them and go.

```
s = 'hi'
print s[1]       ## i
print len(s)     ## 2
print s + ' there' ## hi there
```

Unlike in Java, The operator '+' here does not change numbers automatically or some other types to the string form. The str() function changes values to a string form so that they can be joined with other strings.

```
pi = 3.14
##text = 'The value of pi is ' + pi     ## NO, does not work
text = 'The value of pi is ' + str(pi) ## yes
```

For numbers, the ordinary operators, *, /,+ work in the normal way. We do not have ++ operator but the +=.-= and so on work. If you desire an integer division, it is most appropriate to use 2 slashes—such as in 6//5 is 1—prior to Python 3000, one / does int or integer division with ints anyway; as we move forward though, // is the most preferred way of indicating that you need an integer division.

The operator 'print' prints out a single item or more in Python and then a newline (to inhibit the newline, leave a comma at the close of the items). A 'raw' string literal, prefixed by 'r' passes through without placing any special treatment of the backlashes- thys r'x\nx' is evaluating to the length- 4 string 'x\nx'. A 'u' prefix enables you to do a Unicode string literal- and as you would probably know, Python has numerous other Unicode support features.

```
raw = r'this\t\n and that'
print raw     ## this\t\n and that

multi = """It was the best of times.
It was the worst of times."""
```

String methods

We will now discuss some of the most popular string methods. A method is just like a function only that it runs 'on' an object (more on objects shortly). If the s variable happens to be a string, the code s.lower() thus executes the lower() method on the string object in question and then returns the result.

Look at the following string methods. I will try to include a little bit of description for each.

s.lower(), s.upper(). This one returns the uppercase or lowercase string's version.

s.strip(). Returns a string; the whitespace in this case is removed from the beginning and end.

s.isalpha()/s.isdigit()/s.isspace()... This one checks whether all the string chars are in the different character classes.

s.startswith('other'), s.endswith('other'). It tests or checks whether the string is starting or ending with the other string in question.

s.find('other'). This one runs a search for the other string in question (but not the usual expression) inside s and then returns the initial index where it is beginning or -1 if it's not found.

s.replace('old', 'new'). This one returns a string in which the 'old' occurrences have been substituted by 'new'.

s.split('delim'). It returns a substrings list separated by some delimiter. The delimiter is not some regular expression but a text. Consider 'aaa,bbb,ccc'.split(',') -> ['aaa', 'bbb', 'ccc']. S.split() –without any arguments- splits on all the whitespace chars- as a useful special case.

s.join(list). This is opposite of split(); it joins elements in a given list with the string acting as the delimiter- for instance '---'.join (['aaa', 'bbb', 'ccc']) -> aaa---bbb---ccc

When you do a simple Google search for "Python str," you should see all the str methods on the official website: Python.org string methods.

Python does not have a separate type of character. Rather, there is an expression such as s[8] that returns a string length-1 that contains the character. The string length -1 ensures the operators <=, == are working as you would expect, thus, you usually do not have to know that Python does not have a separate scalar type of char.

The String Slices

The 'slice' syntax is a great way of referring to the sequences' subparts—which is usually lists and strings. The s[start:end] slice represents the elements that start at the starting point and extend up to end , but not including it.

Let's imagine we've got s = 'Hello'

$$Hello$$

$$\begin{array}{ccccc} 0 & 1 & 2 & 3 & 4 \end{array}$$

$$\begin{array}{ccccc} -5 & -4 & -3 & -2 & -1 \end{array}$$

1. s[1:4] is 'ell'. These are the chars that start at index 1 and extend up to index four, without including it

2. s[1:] is 'ello'. It omits either the defaults of the index to the beginning or end of the string.

3. s[:] is 'Hello'. Omitting the two always offers a copy of the entire thing- which is the Pythonic way of copying a sequence such as a list or string

4. s[1:100] is 'ello'. An index that proves too big becomes condensed down to string length

63

The standard index numbers that are zero-based offer easy access to the chars close to the beginning of the string. Alternatively, Python uses negative numbers to offer simple access to the chars at the close of the string. Here s[-1] is the final char 'o' and s[2] is 'l' next to the final char, and so forth. Negative index numbers usually count back from the string's close or end:

1. The last char, that is first from the close is s[-1] is 'o'

2. The fourth from the close is s[-4] is 'e'

3. s[:-3] is 'He' represents going up to, but doesn't include the final three chars

4. s[-3:] is 'llo' beginning with the third char from the close/end and outspreading to the close of the string

As you might guess, it is a straight truism that for any index n, s[:n] + s[n:] == s. Indeed, this works for n negative as well. In different terms, s[:n] and s[n:] always dividing the string into two parts of the string, conserving each and every character. When you get some knowledge about lists, you might realize that slices work neatly with lists as well.

Before continuing, you might want to go through the following topic under strings:

i18n Strings (Unicode)

Python Lists

Python has a large in-built list type known as 'list'. The list literals are usually written inside the square brackets-'[]'. The lists work just like strings – to access data, they use the square brackets and the len() function; the first element is at index 0.

You can also check out the lists docs at the <u>official python</u> <u>website</u>.

```
colors = ['red', 'blue', 'green']
print colors[0]   ## red
print colors[2]   ## green
print len(colors) ## 3
```

Assignment that contains an=on the lists does not make a copy. Rather, assignments make both variables point to the single list in the memory.

```
b = colors   ## Does not copy the list
```

The 'empty list' is simply some empty brackets []. '+' functions to combine two lists, thus [1,2] + [3,4] will produce [1,2,3,4] – this is similar to + with strings.

IN and FOR

In Python, the constructs of 'in' and 'for' are very convenient and you will notice that their first use is with lists. The construct 'for'–for var in lists–is a very easy means to look at every element in a list (or some other collection). During iteration, do not add or take away (remove) from the list.

65

```
squares = [1, 4, 9, 16]
sum = 0
for num in squares:
  sum += num
print sum  ## 30
```

If by any chance you already know the components of the list, you can use a variable name in the loop in order to capture that very information e.g. 'name', 'url' or 'num'. Because there is no other syntax in Python code to remind you of types, what you have to keep straight or focused on is what is going on in your variable names.

The construction 'in' is a simple way to test whether some element is appearing in a list (or another collection)–value in collection–works to test whether the value is still in the collection, and returns true or false.

```
list = ['larry', 'curly', 'moe']
if 'curly' in list:
  print 'yay'
```

The constructs for/in are very popular in Python code and function on data types apart from list, so you only have to memorize their syntax. In addition, you could be having some bits from other languages where you begin iterating over collections manually—where in Python you could just use for/in.

You can also use For/in to work on a string where the string behaves like a list of its chars; therefore, 'for ch in s: print ch' will print all the string chars.

Tuples

Like a list, a tuple is a sequence of values. Normally, the various values stored within a tuple are usually indexed by integers and can be any type. The main variance between tuples and lists is that tuples are actually immutable while lists are not. Moreover, tuples are hashable and comparable, which means that you can actually sort lists of tuples and use the tuples as important values in Python dictionaries.

In terms of syntax, a tuple is a list of values separated by a comma.

```
>>> t = 'a', 'b', 'c', 'd', 'e'
```

Even though it is not necessary, it is common to enclose tuples in parentheses so that it is easy to identify tuples when looking at Python code:

```
>>> t = ('a', 'b', 'c', 'd', 'e')
```

To create a tuple with one element, you have to include the last comma:

```
>>> t1 = ('a',)
>>> type(t1)
```

```
<type 'tuple'>
```

Python perceives ('a') as an expression that has a string in parentheses which evaluates to a string.

```
>>> t2 = ('a')
>>> type(t2)
```

```
<type 'str'>
```

Alternatively, you can construct a tuple using the built-in function tuple. Without an argument, it builds an empty tuple.

```
>>> t = tuple()
>>> print t

()
```

If at all the argument is a sequence–that is string list or tuple– the product of the call to tuple is automatically a tuple containing the sequence element.

```
>>> t = tuple('lupins')
>>> print t

('l', 'u', 'p', 'i', 'n', 's')
```

Since tuple is a name of a constructor, try not to use it as the name of a variable.

Moreover, many list operators work on tuples as well and the bracket operator is responsible for indexing an element:

```
>>> t = ('a', 'b', 'c', 'd', 'e')
>>> print t[0]

'a'
```

The slice operator chooses a range/array of elements.

```
>>> print t[1:3]

('b', 'c')
```

However, if you try modifying a single element of the tuple, you receive an error as follows:

PYTHON PROGRAMMING FOR BEGINNERS

```
>>> t[0] = 'A'
```

TypeError: object doesn't support item assignment

You cannot modify the tuple elements but you can have one tuple replacing another as follows:

```
>>> t = ('A',) + t[1:]
>>> print t
```

('A', 'b', 'c', 'd', 'e')

Dictionaries

Dictionaries are a compound kind that is essentially different from the types of sequences we found in lists, strings, and tuples. They comprise the in-built mapping type of Python. They map keys (these keys can actually be any immutable type), to different values (these values can be of any type e.g. tuple values or the values of a list).

You have to note that in computer science, we dictionaries can also be referred to as associative arrays, symbol tables, and maps. The pairs of values are known as field-value, key-value, name-value, or attribute-values.

Let us look at an example: we will try to create a dictionary that will attempt to translate some English words into Spanish. The keys for this dictionary are strings.

One effective way to create a dictionary is starting with the empty dictionary and adding key-value pairs. A pair of curly braces {} represent the empty dictionary:

```
>>> eng2sp = {}
>>> type(eng2sp)
<class 'dict'>
>>> eng2sp['one'] = 'uno'
>>> eng2sp['two'] = 'dos'

>>> eng2sp['three'] = 'tres'
```

The initial assignment usually generates a dictionary with the name eng2sp. Moreover, any new assignments usually add new/fresh key-value pairs to the initial dictionary. In the usual way, you can print the existing value of the dictionary as follows:

```
>>> print(eng2sp)
```

```
{'three': 'tres', 'one': 'uno', 'two': 'dos'}
```

Commas are used to separate the dictionary's key-value pairs. Each pair has a key as well as a value that is separated by a colon.

The exact organization of the pairs may not necessarily be as you might have expected. As a program, Python determines where the key-value pairs are kept in a dictionary by use of complex algorithms. For this purpose, you can think of this organization as being unpredictable, and thus, you should not try to rely on it; rather, you should try looking up values using a known key.

Another method of creating a dictionary is providing a list of key-value pairs with the same syntax as the earlier output.

```
>>> eng2sp = {'one': 'uno', 'two': 'dos', 'three': 'tres'}
```

Actually, the order you use to write the pairs does not matter since the values in a dictionaries are retrieved with keys and not indices—thus, ordering is not important.

Look at how you can use a key to look up the corresponding value below:

```
>>> eng2sp['two']
'dos'
The key 'two' yields the value 'dos'.
```

The Dictionary Operations

The 'del' statement takes away key-value pairs from dictionaries. For instance, the dictionary below has names of different fruits and the number of each one of them in the inventory:

```
>>> inventory = {'apples': 430, 'bananas': 312, 'oranges': 525,
'pears': 217}
>>> print(inventory)s
```

{'apples': 430, 'bananas': 312, 'pears': 217, 'oranges': 525}

If a person purchases all the pears here, you can take away the entry from the dictionary as follows:

```
>>> del inventory['pears']
>>> print(inventory)
```

{'apples': 430, 'bananas': 312, 'oranges': 525}

Otherwise, if you are expecting some more pears in the coming days, you could just change the value related to the pears.

```
>>> inventory['pears'] = 0
>>> print(inventory)
```

{'apples': 430, 'bananas': 312, 'pears': 0, 'oranges': 525}

The function 'len' works on dictionaries as well; it returns the amount of key-value pairs as follows:

```
>>> len(inventory)
```

4

The operator 'in' returns 'true' when the key shows up in the dictionary and 'false' otherwise:

```
>>> 'pears' in inventory
True
>>> 'blueberries' in inventory
```

False

This operator is undoubtedly very important because looking up on a dictionary's on-existent brings about runtime error.

```
>>> inventory['blueberries']
Traceback (most recent call last):
  File "", line 1, in <module>
KeyError: 'blueberries'

>>>
```

To address the problem we have here, we have the build-in method 'get' to provide a default value that is returned if a key is not accessible.

```
>>> inventory.get('blueberries', 0)
0
>>> inventory.get('bananas', 0)

312
```

The in-built function 'sorted' returns dictionaries keys lists in a sorted method as follows:

```
>>> sorted(inventory)

['apples', 'bananas', 'oranges', 'pears']
```

Decision Making

Decision making is the anticipation of conditions that occur as the program is executed and also the specifying of actions taken with regards to the conditions.

In a program, decisions are used when the program contains conditional choices to guide execution of a code block. For instance- traffic lights have different light colors that light up at different scenarios according to the road conditions or any particular rule.

The decision structures assess different expressions that produce either TRUE or FALSE as the outcome. You have to determine the action you need to take and the statements to execute when the result is either TRUE or FALSE.

Look at the general form of a standard structure of decision making that you will find in most programming languages today:

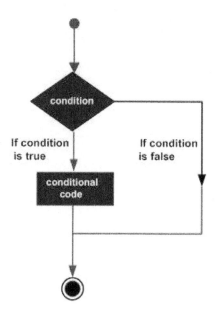

The Python language takes any non-null and non-zero values as TRUE. Thus, if it is null or zero, the program assumes it is a FALSE value. The language offers the decision making statements below:

1. If statements: The "if" statements are made up of Boolean expressions followed by a single statement or more.

2. If...else statements: An optional else statement can follow the if statement–this executes when the Boolean expression is FALSE

3. Nested if statements: You can use a single else if statement or if statement within another else if or if statement.

We'll now go through each one of the decision making in brief:

The single statement suites

If an 'If' clause suite only comprises a single line, it could go on the same line as the header statement.

Look at the following example of a 'one-line if' clause.

```
#!/usr/bin/python

var = 100
if ( var == 100 ) : print "Value of expression is 100"

print "Good bye!"
```

When we execute the code above, it gives out the result below:

Value of expression is 100

Good bye!

If statements

If statements are the simplest decision making statements; their main use is to determine if a particular statement or statement block will be executed or not—that is, if a particular condition is true, then a statement block is executed, otherwise it is not.

The syntax is as follows:

```
if condition:
   # Statements to execute if
   # condition is true
```

The condition after evaluation here is either true or false. The 'if' statement admits Boolean values—so if the value is true, it will then execute the statements beneath it, otherwise it will not. You can actually use condition with bracket ('') as well.

As you know, Python identifies a block using indentation. This means that the block beneath an if statement will be identified as described in the example below:

```
if condition:
    statement1
statement2
```

```
# Here if the condition is true, if block
# will consider only statement1 to be inside
# its block.
```

The flowchart:

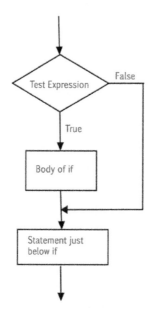

python program to illustrate If statement

```
i = 10
if (i > 15):
    print ("10 is less than 15")
print ("I am Not in if")
```

The Output is:

I am Not in if

Since the condition in the if statement is false, the block beneath the if statement will not be executed as a result.

If-else

Only the if statement informs you that when a condition is true, it will execute a statement block; and if that condition is false, it will not. Even so, what happens in an instance where you want to do something else and yet the condition is false? This calls for the 'else' statement. You can use the else statement together with the if statement to execute a code block when the condition happens to be false.

The syntax is as follows:

```
if (condition):
    # Executes this block if
    # condition is true
else:
    # Executes this block if
    # condition is false
```

Its flowchart:

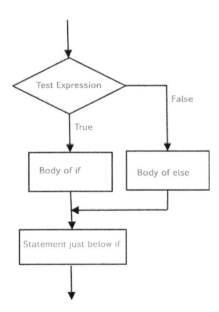

```
# python program to illustrate If else statement
#!/usr/bin/python

i = 20;
if (i < 15):
    print ("i is smaller than 15")
    print ("i'm in if Block")
else:
    print ("i is greater than 15")
    print ("i'm in else Block")
print ("i'm not in if and not in else Block")
```

The output is:

i is greater than 15
i'm in else Block
i'm not in if and not in else Block

The code block succeeding the else statement is then executed since the condition existing in the if statement is false.

Nested-if

A nested-if is simply an if statement that is target of some other if statement. The nested if statements refers to an if statement within another if statement. Indeed, the Python language lets us nest the if statements inside the if statements—that is, you can place an if statement within another.

The syntax is as follows:

```
if (condition1):
    # Executes when condition1 is true
    if (condition2):
        # Executes when condition2 is true
    # if Block is end here
# if Block is end here
```

...and the flow chart:

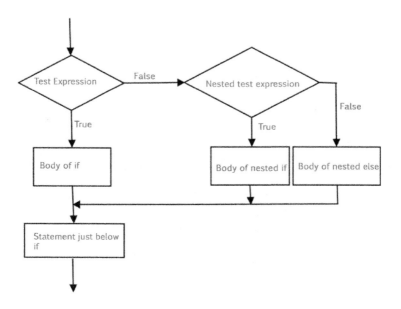

```
# python program to illustrate nested If statement
#!/usr/bin/python
i = 10
if (i == 10):
   #  First if statement
   if (i < 15):
      print ("i is smaller than 15")
   # Nested - if statement
   # Will only be executed if statement above
   # it is true
   if (i < 12):
      print ("i is smaller than 12 too")
   else:
      print ("i is greater than 15")
```

The output is as follows:

i is smaller than 15
i is smaller than 12 too

Loops in Python

Loops are a very important part of Python just as much as they are in other programming languages because they aid the repeated execution of a code block. As a programmer, you will come face to face with situations where you will have to use some bit of code repeatedly but you do not want to put down the same line of code many times.

Generally, statements are executed in sequences: the first statement in a function is executed first then followed by the second one and so on. As I mentioned, you will have situations where you have to execute a block of code a couple of times. Programming languages offers you different structures of control to enable execution of more complicated paths.

Loop statements give us the opportunity to execute a statements or collection of statements many times.

Loop Flow Diagram

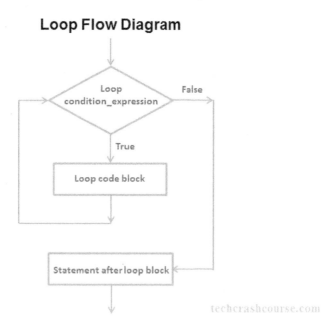

Python offers the following types of loops in order to manage looping requirements.

1. While loop: This loop repeats statements or collections of statements if a condition in question is TRUE; it runs a test on the condition before it executes the loop body.

2. For loop: This one executes sequences of statements many times before abbreviating the code that handles the loop variable.

3. Nested loops: you can generally use a single or more loops within another while, do while or for loop.

The while loop

The while loop is one of the first loops you will definitely come across when you are learning Python; it is arguably the most intuitive one to comprehend. When you look at the name loop, you will understand pretty quickly that the other word 'while' has something to do with a 'period of time' or 'interval'; and as you obviously know already, the word loop refers to a piece of code you execute in repetition.

Having that in mind, you are ready for the definition below of while loop:

A while loop is a concept of programming that when implemented, executes a code repeatedly as long as a particular condition still holds true. You may be able to see three highlighted components in the definition above that you require to construct the Python's while loop:

1. The keyword while

2. A condition translating to either false or true

3. A code block you need to execute repeatedly

That is all it actually takes.

Creating A While Loop In Python

This far, you know what you require to create a while loop; you now need to observe a real-life example of the application of the while loop before you start experimenting with it. Look at the example below:

```
# Take user input
number = 2

# Condition of the while loop
while number < 5 :
    print("Thank you")
    # Increment the value of the variable "number by 1"
    number = number+1
Thank you
Thank you
Thank you
```

In the example above, you can see a simple while loop: the three components you read about before are all present–if you are keen, you will notice it. These components include the while keyword followed by a condition translating to either false or true (number <5), as well as a code block you want to execute repeatedly:

print("Thank you")

number = number + 1

If you look into the code above in more detail, you will notice the presence of a 'number' variable that you store an integer 2 in. Because of the fact that the value in 'number' is less than five, you print out 'thank you' and then increase the 'number' value with one. As the value in 'number' remains less than five, you keep executing the two code lines contained inside the while loop as follows:

"Thank you"

"Thank you"

You print 'thank you' out two times more before 'number' value is equivalent to five and the condition no longer evaluates to 'true'. Since the condition is now evaluating to 'false', you will exit the while loop and go on with your program if it has more code. In this case, we do not have any more code and thus, the program will stop.

The example above is basic. You can also include conditionals or put differently, an if condition, so that it becomes even more customized. Consider the example below:

```python
# Take user input
number = 2

# Condition of the while loop
while number < 5 :
  # Find the mod of 2
  if number%2 == 0:
    print("The number "+str(number)+" is even")
  else:
    print("The number "+str(number)+" is odd")

  # Increment `number` by 1
  number = number+1
The number 2 is even
The number 3 is odd

The number 4 is even
```

For Loop

You can approach the for loop in the same way you would a while loop. As you may probably expect, the component 'for' in 'for loop' refers to something you perform a given number of times.

With all the above in consideration, you can define the for loop as follows:

A for loop is a concept in programming that executes a piece of code over and over again (when it is implemented) 'for' a given number of times according to a sequence.

Unlike the while loop, here, we do not have any condition actively involved–you only execute a code a number of times repeatedly. In simpler terms, as the while loop continues to execute the block of code present within it, only until the condition is 'true' does the for loop execute the code present inside it just for a particular number of times. The 'number of times' I'm talking about is settled by a sequence, or an organized list of things.

Let's now delve into the pieces below that you require to create a for loop:

As opposed to the while loop, the for loop does not have actively involved condition—all you need to do in this case is to repeatedly execute a piece of code. Let me put it in another way; although while loop has a tendency of executing the code within it until the condition is actually True, on the contrary, the for loop usually executes the block of code that is within it for a predetermined number of times. What determines the 'number of times' is an ordered list of things or a sequence.

1. The 'for' keyword

2. The 'in' keyword

3. The code you particularly need to execute repeatedly

4. A variable

5. The function 'range()' (which is an in-built function in the Python library) to assist us build a sequence of numbers

Python's for Loops

```
# Print "Thank you" 5 times
for number in range(5):
    print("Thank you")
Thank you
Thank you
Thank you
Thank you

Thank you
```

You can see above that the components you saw in the section above return in the small example here of a for loop in the Python language: the keyword 'for', the 'number' variable and function 'range()' as well as the code you need to execute many times, 'print("Thank you")'.

That is not hard to understand, right?

We will try considering one more example of a for loop where we shall use two variables to describe the control flow:

```
languages = ['R', 'Python', 'Scala', 'Java', 'Julia']

for index in range(len(languages)):
    print('Current language:', languages[index])
Current language: R
Current language: Python
Current language: Scala
Current language: Java

Current language: Julia
```

It is clear that you begin the loop using the 'for' keyword. After that, you use the variables 'languages' and 'index', the keyword 'in' and the function 'range()' in order to build a number sequence. Moreover, you see that in this case, you use the function 'len()' as well since the list 'languages' is not numerical. The code that you ought to repeatedly execute is really just a print statement with the name below:

```
print('Current language :', languages[index])
```

As for the above loop, you ought to express that for each index within the range 'len(languages)', you mean to print the data science language. Len(languages) at the moment is 5, thus, the statement could be put down this way as well:

```
for index in range(5):
    print('Current language:', languages[index])
Current language: R
Current language: Python
Current language: Scala
Current language: Java
Current language: Julia
```

Once again, this offers you the same result.

Nested loops

You can try including more while loop within your current code which is referred to as a nested loop.

```
# Take user input
number = 2

# condition of the while loop
while number < 5 :
    # condition of the nested while loop
    while number % 2 == 0:

        print("The number "+ str(number)+" is even")
```

In the example above, we have another while loop that is 'nested' within the outer loop. The inner loop places in another check to see whether the "number % (mod) 2 is 0."

Put differently, it looks at whether the number is even and then prints the following statement: 'the number is even.'

Nonetheless, there is a catch; when you look close enough, you can see that just like the earlier code, the statement 'number=number+1' is missing here. The variable value stays the same each time as well as the code keys in an infinite loop because you are not even increasing the variable number anywhere. This means that whenever it enters the loop, it actually never gets to leave. Instead, it prints the statement infinitely since the 'number' variable will constantly be set to 2. This number is, definitely, less than five, and is an even number.

We will now look at how a nested loop would appear:

```
# Print the below statement 3 times
for number in range(3) :
    print("-------------------------------------------")
    print("I am outer loop iteration "+str(number))
    # Inner loop
    for another_number in range(5):
        print("**************************")
        print("I am inner loop iteration "+str(another_number))
-------------------------------------------
I am outer loop iteration 0
**************************
I am inner loop iteration 0
**************************
I am inner loop iteration 1
**************************
I am inner loop iteration 2
**************************
I am inner loop iteration 3
**************************
I am inner loop iteration 4
```

```
----------------------------------------------
I am outer loop iteration 1
***************************
I am inner loop iteration 0
***************************
I am inner loop iteration 1
***************************
I am inner loop iteration 2
***************************
I am inner loop iteration 3
***************************
I am inner loop iteration 4
----------------------------------------------
I am outer loop iteration 2
***************************
```

The code above is just a modified form of the initial for loop example. You need to note the use of a second for loop within the outer loop.

You can now move on to execute the code.

Here, you will discover that the control usually enters the very first 'for loop' while the value of the variable number has a 0. The initial print statement is printed first after which the control inputs the next (the second) for loop where the variable 'another_number' value has 0 as its initial. The initial print statement in the subsequent loop is printed a single time.

At this time, the control returns the for loop on the inside once more and the 'another_number' value is initialized to the following integer once more and after that comes the printing of the statement within the 'print()' function.

The process mentioned above continues until the control goes through the close of the function 'range', which in this case is 5, and then the control goes back to the outmost loop, starts the 'number' variable to the following integer, prints the statement within the function 'print()' and visits the inner loop before repeating all the steps until it traverses the function 'range()'.

This control journey from the outmost loop, the crossing of the inner loop, and then back to the very outer for loop once more goes on until the whole range has been covered by the control, which is thrice in this case.

Having known as much as you can know about nested loops, try writing a Python program to create the pattern below using a nested for loop.

```
*
*  *
*  *  *
*  *  *  *
*  *  *  *  *
*  *  *  *
*  *  *
*  *
*
```

Initialize the first five rows

n = _

Start the loop to print the first five rows

for i in range(_):

    for j in range(i):

        print('* ', end="")

    print(")

The Loop Control Statements

The loop control statements alter the execution from its regular sequence. In instances where execution leaves a scope, the entire automatic objects made in the scope are destroyed.

Python will support the control statements below:

1. Break statement: This one ends the loop statement before transferring the execution to the statement

2. Continue statement: It makes the loop skip the rest of its body and retest its condition immediately prior to reiterating.

3. Pass statement: In Python, this kind of statement is used when a statement is syntactically needed but you do not want execution of any code or command.

Read more on loop control statements here.

About User-Defined Functions

Functions are popular to all existing programming languages; you can define it as a block of reusable code that can perform particular tasks.

In Python, to define functions means getting to know both user-defined and built-in types of functions first. The built-in functions are typically a part of the Python packages and libraries while the user-defined functions are the creations of developers looking to meet particular requirements. All the functions in Python are treated as objects. This makes Python more flexible a language when compared to other high-level languages.

In this section, we will be looking at user-defined Python functions. To understand the concept fully, you will learn how you can implement them by writing examples of code.

Before we jump into coding, we will first look at other essential concepts.

The Importance of User-Defined Functions in Python

Generally, you can write functions that are user-defined as a developer or borrow a third-party library. This means that the functions that are user defined can in turn act as a third party library for developers and other users. Depending on how and when they are used, the user-defined functions contain particular advantages.

Consider the points below:

1. The user-defined functions are simply reusable blocks of code that you only need to write once but can use many times. You can use them in other applications as well.

2. These functions are extremely useful–from writing specific business logic to common utilities. You can also modify these functions per requirement.

3. The code is particularly easy to maintain, well organized and developer friendly. This means it offers support for the modular design approach.

4. Since you can write the user-defined functions independently, the project tasks can be distributed for quick development of applications.

5. Lastly, user-defined functions that are thoroughly written and well defined generally ease the process of application development.

With this basic understanding of the advantages, you are now ready to look at the various function arguments in Python.

The Function Arguments

In Python, user-defined functions could take four types of arguments. However, the argument meanings and their types are predefined and therefore unchangeable. As a developer though, you can instead follow these predefined rules to create your own custom functions.

Discussed below are the four argument types and their rules.

1: Default arguments

As you should already know, Python has a distinct way of not only representing syntax but also function arguments' default values. The default values show that the function argument will take the value if there is no argument value passed during function call. The default value is typically assigned with the assignment operator '='.

Look at the typical syntax below for default argument. In this case, the 'msg' paramenter contains a default value 'Hello!'

Function definition

```
def defaultArg( name, msg = "Hello!"):
```

The functional call

```
defaultArg( name)
```

2: Required arguments

The required arguments are simply the mandatory or obligatory arguments of a function. These values of the argument should be passed in the right number and order during the call function.

Look at the typical syntax for a necessary argument function below:

Functional definition

```
def requiredArg (str, num):
```
_____

The functional call

```
requiredArg ("Hello", 12)
```

3: Keyword arguments

These are important and applicable for the functional calls in Python. During the function call, these keywords are mentioned together with their agreeing values. The function argument is very important for mapping these keywords to enable the function to identify the corresponding values with a lot of ease even when the order is not upheld all through the function call.

Look at the syntax below for keyword arguments

Function definition

def keywordArg(name, role):

The function call

keywordArg(name = "Tom", role = "Manager")

or

keywordArg(role = "Manager", name = "Tom")

4: The variable number of arguments

When you do not know the exact number of arguments to be passed to a function, this will be very convenient. Alternatively, you can have a design where any number of arguments can be passed according to the requirement.

Look at the syntax below that represents this kind of function call:

Function definition

def varlengthArgs(*varargs):

The function call

varlengthArgs(30,40,50,60)

At this point, you should be having a good idea about the different types of arguments in Python.

Let us now look at the steps you can take to write a user-defined function.

How to Write User-Defined Functions in Python

The following are the basic steps you can take to write Python user-defined functions. You will need to incorporate more steps as required for extra functionalities.

1. Step 1: Declare that function using the 'def' keyword accompanied by the function name.

2. Step 2: Write the arguments within the function's opening and closing parentheses.

3. Step 3: Add the statements of the program that will be executed

4. Step 4: Finish the function using / without the return statement.

In the example below, I have described a typical syntax to define functions:

```
def userDefFunction (arg1, arg2, arg3 ...):
    program statement1
    program statement3
    program statement3
    ....

    return;
```

Examples of Code

We will now go ahead and use four examples for all the four function arguments discussed above.

Example 1: Default arguments

The code below is a snippet representing a default argument example. The code is written in a script known as defArg.py

The first listing in the default argument example

```
def defArgFunc( empname, emprole = "Manager" ):
  print ("Emp Name: ", empname)
  print ("Emp Role ", emprole)
  return;
print("Using default value")
defArgFunc(empname="Nick")
print("************************")
print("Overwriting default value")

defArgFunc(empname="Tom",emprole = "CEO")
```

You can now run the script file as described below. You will receive an output is follows:

```
E:\Python>python defArg.py
Using default value
Emp Name:   Nick
Emp Role   Manager
************************
Overwriting default value
Emp Name:   Tom
Emp Role   CEO

E:\Python>
```

Example 2: Required arguments

The code below is a snippet representing an example of a required argument. The code is written in a script known as reqArg.py

The second listing in the required argument example

```
def reqArgFunc( empname):
  print ("Emp Name: ", empname)
  return;
print("Not passing required arg value")
reqArgFunc()
print("Now passing required arg value")

reqArgFunc("Hello")
```

You can now run the code; first, do not pass the required argument and you will get the following output displayed:

```
E:\Python>python reqArg.py
Not passing required arg value
Traceback (most recent call last):
  File "reqArg.py", line 6, in <module>
    reqArgFunc()
TypeError: reqArgFunc() missing 1 required positional argument: 'empname'

E:\Python>
```

Now comment out the function call reqArgFunc() in the script and then run the code using the required argument. You will get the output below:

```
E:\Python>python reqArg.py
Now passing required arg value
Emp Name:  Hello

E:\Python>
```

Example 3: keyword arguments

97

The example below describes a snippet of keyword argument code. The code has been written in a script file known as KeyArg.py

The third listing in the Keyword argument example:

```
def keyArgFunc(empname, emprole):
  print ("Emp Name: ", empname)
  print ("Emp Role: ", emprole)
  return;
print("Calling in proper sequence")
keyArgFunc(empname = "Nick",emprole = "Manager" )
print("Calling in opposite sequence")

keyArgFunc(emprole = "Manager",empname = "Nick")
```

As always, you can now run the script file as described below. The output you will receive is as follows:

```
E:\Python>python keyArg.py
Calling in proper sequence
Emp Name:  Nick
Emp Role:  Manager
Calling in opposite sequence
Emp Name:  Nick
Emp Role:  Manager

E:\Python>_
```

Example 4: Variable number of arguments

The snippet below is a code showing an example of variable length argument. The code has been written in a script known as var.Arg.py

The fourth listing of a variable length argument:

```
def varLenArgFunc(*varvallist ):
  print ("The Output is: ")
  for varval in varvallist:
    print (varval)
  return;
```

98

```
print("Calling with single value")
varLenArgFunc(55)
print("Calling with multiple values")

varLenArgFunc(50,60,70,80)
```

When you run the code, you will get the output below:

```
E:\Python>python varArg.py
Calling with single value
The Output is:
55
Calling with multiple values
The Output is:
50
60
70
80

E:\Python>_
```

About Coding Style

At this point, you are set to write longer and more complex pieces of Python. Thus, it is an opportune time to talk something about the coding style.

Most current programming languages are typically written or formatted in various styles, some of which are more readable. You need to note that it is always a good idea to ensure your code is easy for other people to read; adopting a good coding style thus helps.

When it comes to Python, it appears that most projects adhere to PEP 8 as the style guide. It (PEP 8) promotes a tremendously readable and less repulsing (to the eye) coding style. At some point, every Python developer should read it.

Look at some of the most important point I have extracted for you in this respect.

1. Always try using 4-space indentations without tabs. This is because 4 spaces provide a nice compromise between little indentation (as it allows better nesting depth) and pretty large indentation (as it is simpler to read). Tabs only bring in confusion and its best to leave them out.

2. Wrap lines to ensure they do not surpass 79 characters. This is particularly important because it helps the users with tiny displays; on bigger displays, it enables having a number of files side by side.

3. Separate functions and classes and functions with blank lines; this also includes the larger blocks of code within functions.

4. When you can, try putting comments on their own line.

5. Use docstrings

6. Use spaces around the operators as well as after commas– this should however not be the case within bracketing constructs: a = f(1, 2) + g(3, 4).

7. Name your functions and classes as consistently as possible; conventionally, use (for the functions and methods) lower_case_with_underscores. Make it a habit to be using self as the first method argument's name.

8. Lastly, if you want your code to be used in international environments, avoid encodings. The best in any case is plain ASCII.

Practice Projects: The Python Projects for Your Practice

We will now practice what we have learnt so far by creating some simple projects. This is definitely the best part!

A Text-Based Game

To learn a bit more about how Python really works and become prepared for more advanced programming, you can try looking at game logic.

In this section, you will also get to learn a bit about the general structure of computer programs by creating a text-based game where the player and the computer roll a virtual die and between the two, the one with the highest roll is the winner.

Plan the game

Before you write code, it is essential to think about what you intend to write. Most programmers write simple documentation (<u>read more</u>) before starting to write code to have an end to program toward.

Here is how the dice program might appear if you had the documentation shipped together with the game:

1. Start the dice game and roll by pressing enter or return.

2. You will see the results printed out to the screen

3. You will see a prompt asking you to roll once more or quit.

While this is a simple game, the documentation informs you so much about what you have to do. For instance, it informs you that you require the components below to write the game.

1. The player: You require a person to play the game

2. Al: The computer also has to roll a die; otherwise, the player does not have anyone to lose or win to.

3. Random number: The regular die with six sides offers a random number in between 1 and 6.

4. The Operator: Easy math can make a comparison of the numbers to see the higher one.

5. The win or lose message

6. A prompt to quit or play once again

Make a dice game alpha

A few programs begin with all their features; thus, the first version only implements the fundamentals.

Well, a variable is a value that can change; variables are common in Python. Each time we require our programs to recall something, we use variables. Actually, nearly all information that code will work with gets to be stored in variables. Take the equation Y+6=45 as an example; the variable is x since the x letter acts as a placeholder for a value.

An integer on the other hand is a number that can be negative or positive. For instance, -1 and 1 are integers, much like 34, 64 or even 29109.

In Python, variables are simple to build and simple to work with; therefore, this first version of the game uses dual variables that include ai and player.

Type the code below into a new text file with the name 'dice_alpha.py'

```
import random


    player = random.randint(1,6)

    ai = random.randint(1,6)


    if player > ai :

        print("You win")  # notice indentation

    else:

        print("You lose")
```

Now launch your game to see if it really works.

This simple version of the game actually works very well; it achieves the game's basic goals, even though it does not feel much like a game. As a player, you do not know what you rolled or even what the computer rolled and the game ends even if you, the player, would love to play once more.

This is very normal in the initial version of software known as 'alpha version'. I believe you are now confident that you will achieve the main thing, which is rolling a die; and so, it is time you added to the program.

Improve the game

In this stage, or the second version known as beta of the game, we will do some improvements to make it look and feel a little more like a game.

Describe your results

Rather than just informing a player whether he/she won or did not win, it could be more interesting if the player knew what he or she rolled. You can thus try to make the following changes to your code:

```
player = random.randint(1,6)

    print("You rolled " + player)


    ai = random.randint(1,6)


    print("The computer rolled " + ai)
```

NOTE: At this point, if you run the game, it will only crash since it thinks you are trying to do some math. According to it, you are trying to add the letters that you rolled and the number presently kept in the player variable.

You have to inform Python to treat the numbers in the player as well as the AI variables as though they were some word in a sentence (or a string) as opposed to an integer or number in some math equation.

Make the following changes to the code:

```
    player = random.randint(1,6)

    print("You rolled " + str(player) )


    ai = random.randint(1,6)


    print("The computer rolled " + str(ai) )
```

Now run the game so that you view the result. Next, slow it down.

Computers are quick; human beings can undeniably be quick, but when you are dealing with games, it is usually better to create some suspense. You can use the time function within Python to slow the game down for the parts containing suspense.

```python
import random

import time


player = random.randint(1,6)

print("You rolled " + str(player) )


ai = random.randint(1,6)

print("The computer rolls...." )

time.sleep(2)

print("The computer has rolled a " + str(player) )


if player > ai :

    print("You win")  # notice indentation

else:

    print("You lose")
```

Now launch the game to run tests to the changes.

Try detecting the ties

If you play the game enough, you will soon discover that while the game appears to be working properly, it has a bug; this means that it does not know what it should do when the computer and player roll a similar number.

Python uses == to view if a value is equivalent to another; note that these are two signs and not one. When you use one of them, the language will think you are creating a new variable— even though you are trying to do math.

If you desire to have more than the two options, that is lose or win, use of the keyword 'elif' which means 'else if'—I believe you remember how it works. This will allow the code to see whether any one of a couple of results is true instead of only checking whether just one thing is true.

Now modify the code as follows:

```python
if player > ai :

    print("You win")  # notice indentation

elif player == ai:

    print("Tie game.")

else:

    print("You lose")
```

Now launch your game a couple of times to check whether you can tie the computer's roll.

Program the last release

Your dice game's beta release is functional and feels so much more like a game than the alpha. Now you can go ahead to create the very first python function for your last release.

Simply put, a function is a group of code you can implore as a separate unit. The thing is; functions are very vital because many applications usually have a large amount of code but the entire code does not have to run at the same time. Functions allow you to start an application and control what occurs and when.

Now change your code to the following:

```python
import random
import time


def dice():
    player = random.randint(1,6)
    print("You rolled " + str(player) )


    ai = random.randint(1,6)
    print("The computer rolls....")
    time.sleep(2)
    print("The computer has rolled a " + str(player) )


    if player > ai :
        print("You win") # notice indentation
    else:
        print("You lose")
```

This version of the game asks the player if he wants to quit the game once he has played. If the player responds with a y or Y, it calls the exit function within Python and the game quits.

What is more important is that you have created dice, your own function. The dice function does not run immediately. Actually, if you try your game here, it will not crash but will not also exactly run. If you want to make the dice function really do something, you have to 'call it' - in your program code.

Now add the loop at the foot of your current code. The two first lines are solely for context and emphasizing what gets indented and what does not. You need to become more observant on indentation.

```
    else:

        print("I did not understand that. Playing again.")


    # main loop

    while True:

        print("Press return to roll your die.")

        roll = input()


        dice()
```

The code block 'while true' will run first. Since by definition True is always true, the code block will run until the Python program asks it to quit.

The block of code 'while True' is a loop. It will first prompt the user to begin the game, and then it shall call your dice function. This is exactly how the game begins. When the dice function is done, the loop will run once more or exit, depending on how the player answered the prompt.

The most common means to code an application is using a loop to run the program. The loop makes sure the application remains open as long as the computer user requires to use the functions inside the application.

Game 2: Mad Libs Generator

Mad Libs is some kind of program where you create a story with a number of words missing–you could also use a pre-built template for the same. You then have to work out the part of speech—whether adjective, noun, adverb, and so on—that would be sensible in each of the blanks.

After that, you request folks to offer you a word that goes with the given parts of speech. Lastly, you fill in the blanks using their answers, and then read out their new funny story.

This project is one that really gets you thinking about how to manipulate or control user-inputted data; normally, the fun of the game is to come up with wacky stories!

Here is an example:

If you remember the "Mary had a little lamb" song/story, I would create it in Mad Libs this way:

I say: give me an adjective

You say: careless

I say: name one animal

You say: goat

I say: name one body part

You say: nose

I say: give me one adjective

You say: lively

Now look at the Mad Libs version of the 'Mary Had a Little Lamb' story

"Mary had a careless goat

Its nose was lively as snow…"

As you would expect, everyone is rolling on the floor laughing and   bewildered!

Create the story

The first thing you have to do is construct a Mad Libs story. You can make up your own story or use a poem, song lyrics, or nursery rhyme.

You also have to include blank spaces in your story for the missing words to correspond with the Mad Libs format; you also have to determine the parts of speech, i.e. pronoun, noun, verb, adjective and so on, belonging to each blank.

Look at the example below using the famous 'Humpty Dumpty' nursery rhyme.

(Name of the person) Dumpty (a verb written in past tense) on a wall

(Name of the person) Dumpty had an/a (adjective) fall.

All the king's (animal in plural) and the (the profession)'s men

Could not put (name of the person) together again

The example above has five variables that include the name of the person, the verb in past tense, adjective, an animal in plural, and profession. I am using the term 'variable' here because since you know what it means already, it is easier to understand when we begin working in Python.

The variables

To convert your story into an operational program, you first need to set up the items to fill in the blanks for the user – by user I mean the person who will be running and responding to the program. To achieve that, just use the following format:

```
variable_name = raw_input ("The content you want the user to respond to.")
```

The purple words are ones that you will change; the other parts comprise Python formatting which you have to maintain. Here is the example I would consider using from a 'Humpty Dumpty' story: The words written in purple are the words you will change. The rest of it is Python formatting that you have to maintain.

Here is an example I would use from my "Humpty Dumpty" story:

```
persons_name = raw_input ("Give the name of a person.")
```

There are some important things I have to remind you when setting your questions though. First, the variable name (the one coming before the equal sign) cannot have a space separating it; thus, if you tried using person's name, it would not work; rather, you can use an underscore.

Additionally, you have to give every one of your variables different names. For instance, you are requesting for three nouns in your story. For your program to work properly, each one of these nouns requires a distinct variable name. To make things simple, you can call also refer to them as noun 1, noun 2 and noun 3. For example:

```
noun1 = raw_input("Name a noun.")
noun2 = raw_input("Name another noun.")
noun3 = raw_input("Name yet another noun.")
```

One more important thing: remember that the punctuation you are going to use has to match the format I have described for you. If you overlook the parentheses or forget the quotation marks, the program will not work well. Ensure your punctuation is right and you are sure about it.

Before you get into the next section of this program, try to run the program you have so far. If you have typed everything properly, the program will ask you to answer every question. Now go ahead. Answer every question to see what follows.

Now, the story

After answering all the questions, you probably noted that not a lot happened. That is because you have not added the answers to your story. We will take care of that now.

At this point, you want to write your story and inform the program to take the answers of the user to the questions and replace the blanks in the story. The format to do that is as follow:

```
print "This is your story right here. %s The percent signs
represent the blanks in your %s story. They are replaced by the
variables within the %s parentheses that follow the stuff in
quotation marks." % (variable_name1. variable_name2.
variable_name3)
```

Once again, the purple words represent the sections you will change based on your story's needs. The items written in black on the other hand need to appear as they are so that Python understands what to do. For the Humpty Dumpty story, I would write the following:

```
print "%s Dumpty %s on a wall. %s Dumpty had a/n %s fall. All
the king's %s and all the %s's men couldn't put %s together again."
% (persons_name, verb, persons_name, adjective, animal,
profession, persons_name)
```

The addendum

You need to note that I used the person's name many times; I only repeated it multiple times in the variable list in the parentheses so that the program knows where to place it in the story. Moreover, you must have noticed that the story went on and on, spreading out way across the page. If you do not want that to happen, you can inform Python to continue your text on the subsequent line. To do that, insert a backlash and then press Enter on the keyboard anytime you need to break to the following line as follows:

```
print "This story is getting really long. I mean, it's getting so long
that it is bleeding across the page. Arrgh! \
Okay, I put in a backslash so that it wouldn't be so long because,
man, it was getting really long, wasn't \
it?"
```

Another thing; if your output/result is on your screen's right side, and it is too squished together (or simply put, you want to add in the blank lines), simply add the word 'print' in areas where you want a blank line.

For instance, you can write the following:

```
noun = raw_input("Name a noun.")
print
adjective = raw_input("Name an adjective.")
print
verb = raw_input("Name a verb.")
```

In the output on your screen, it will look like this:

Name a noun.

Name an adjective.

Name a verb.

This is different from what it would have otherwise appeared

Name a noun.
Name an adjective.
Name a verb.

A Simple Calculator Program

In this tutorial, we are going to learn how to create a very simple command line calculator using Python. There are definitely numerous opportunities to improve the code and create a better calculator but this basic model is a great place to start.

In this project, you need to note that you will need to know about the following:

1. Variables

2. Math operators

3. Conditional statements

4. Functions

Prompt the users for input

Calculators are best when a person is providing equations for the computer to crack. You will begin by writing your program at the time when a person enters numbers he would like the computer to use.

To achieve this, the 'input()' function in Python that takes user-generated input from the keyboard will come in handy. Within the parentheses of the function 'input()', you can pass a string to be able to prompt the user. You will assign the user input to a variable.

For purposes of this program, you will want the user to key in 2 numbers and thus, you need the program to actually prompt the user to enter 2 numbers. In this case, whenever asking for input, you have to insert a space right at the end of the string so that you have some space left between the user input then the prompting string.

number_1 = input('Enter your first number: ')

number_2 = input('Enter your second number: ')

Once you write the two lines, save the program before running it. You can name it calculator.py and in the terminal window, run the program in the programming environment with the 'python calculator,py' command. You have to be able to type into the terminal window to respond to every prompt.

Output
Enter your first number: 5

Enter your second number: 7

When you run the program a couple times and vary your input, you will realize that you can input what you want when

116

prompted–this includes symbols, words, whitespace, or the enter key. This is for the simple reason that 'input()' takes in data as strings and does not know that you are searching for a number.

You have two reasons to use a number in the program:

1. To let the program do arithmetic calculations

2. To confirm that the user input is indeed a numerical string

Depending on the needs of your calculator, you may need to change the string coming in from the function 'input()' to a float or an integer. In your case, whole numbers correspond to the purpose and so, you will wrap the function 'input()' in the function 'int()' to change the input into the integer data type.

calculator.py

```
number_1 = int(input('Enter your first number: '))

number_2 = int(input('Enter your second number: '))
```

If you now put two integers, you will not run into an error.

```
Output
Enter your first number: 23

Enter your second number: 674
```

However, if you enter symbols, letters, or other non-integers, you will see the error below:

```
Output
Enter your first number: sammy
Traceback (most recent call last):
  File "testing.py", line 1, in <module>
    number_1 = int(input('Enter your first number: '))

ValueError: invalid literal for int() with base 10: 'sammy'
```

117

This far, you have been able to establish two variables to keep user input in terms of integer data types. You can also experiment with changing the input to floats.

Add the operators

Before you can finish your program, you have to add four math operators. These include:

1. Addition +

2. Subtraction −

3. Multiplication *

4. Division /

As you create your program, you want to ensure each part is working properly. Here, you are going to begin by establishing the addition. You will add both numbers inside a print function so that the person using the calculator can see the result (output).

calculator.py

```
number_1 = int(input('Enter your first number: '))
number_2 = int(input('Enter your second number: '))


print(number_1 + number_2)
```

Now run the program and ensure to key in 2 numbers whenever the program prompts you to enter 2 numbers (just as you would expect users to).

Output
Enter your first number: 8
Enter your second number: 3

11

The output is showing you that the program is functioning properly; try adding a bit more context so that the user remains fully informed all through the program's runtime. To do that, you will try to use string formatters to help you format the text properly and offer feedback. You want the user to get confirmation about the numbers he is entering as well as the operator used besides the result given.

calculator.py

```
number_1 = int(input('Enter your first number: '))
number_2 = int(input('Enter your second number: '))

print('{} + {} = '.format(number_1, number_2))
print(number_1 + number_2)
```

At this point, running the program will give you some additional output that will enable the user to confirm the arithmetic expression performed by the program.

```
Output
Enter your first number: 90
Enter your second number: 717
90 + 717 =

807
```

The user will get more feedback because of using the string formatters.

You can now include the other operators to your program using the same format you have used for the addition:

calculator.py

```
number_1 = int(input('Enter your first number: '))
number_2 = int(input('Enter your second number: '))

# Addition
print('{} + {} = '.format(number_1, number_2))
print(number_1 + number_2)
```

```
# Subtraction
print('{} - {} = '.format(number_1, number_2))
print(number_1 - number_2)

# Multiplication
print('{} * {} = '.format(number_1, number_2))
print(number_1 * number_2)

# Division
print('{} / {} = '.format(number_1, number_2))

print(number_1 / number_2)
```

According to the program above, the other operators have been added; when you run the program, it will execute all the above operations. Nonetheless, you want to limit the program such that it will only perform a single operation at a time. This requires conditional statements.

Add conditional statements

With the calculator.py program, you want to allow the user to select among the various operators. Thus, let us begin by appending some information to the program, together with a choice to be made so that the individual knows what to do.

You will write a string on a couple of different lines with triple quotes.

```
'''
Please type in the math operation you would like to complete:
+ for addition
- for subtraction
* for multiplication
/ for division
'''
```

You are using every operator symbol so that the users make a choice; thus, if the user desires a division, he will type /.

However, you could select any symbols you want such as b for subtraction or 1 for addition.

Since you are asking users to provide input, you want to incorporate the function 'input()'. You will add the string within the function 'input()' before passing the value of that input to a variable known as 'operation'.

```
calculator.py
operation = input('''
Please type in the math operation you would like to complet
+ for addition
- for subtraction
* for multiplication
/ for division
''')

number_1 = int(input('Enter your first number: '))
number_2 = int(input('Enter your second number: '))

print('{} + {} = '.format(number_1, number_2))
print(number_1 + number_2)

print('{} - {} = '.format(number_1, number_2))
print(number_1 - number_2)

print('{} * {} = '.format(number_1, number_2))
print(number_1 * number_2)

print('{} / {} = '.format(number_1, number_2))
print(number_1 / number_2)
```

If you run your program here, it will not really matter what you put in at the initial prompt; thus, just add your conditional statements within the program. Given the manner in which you have structured your program, the 'if' statement will appear where the addition is conducted. Also, you will have a 3 else-elif or if statements for every one of the other operators; the 'else' statement will be fixed in place to be able to handle an error if the individual did not add an operator symbol.

```
calculator.py
operation = input('"
Please type in the math operation you would like to complete:
+ for addition
- for subtraction
* for multiplication
/ for division
'")

number_1 = int(input('Enter your first number: '))
number_2 = int(input('Enter your second number: '))

if operation == '+':
    print('{} + {} = '.format(number_1, number_2))
    print(number_1 + number_2)

elif operation == '-':
    print('{} - {} = '.format(number_1, number_2))
    print(number_1 - number_2)

elif operation == '*':
    print('{} * {} = '.format(number_1, number_2))
    print(number_1 * number_2)

elif operation == '/':
    print('{} / {} = '.format(number_1, number_2))
    print(number_1 / number_2)

else:
    print('You have not typed a valid operator, please run the program
again.')
```

The user, in the process of walking through this program, is prompted to add an operation symbol. For instance, the user enters * for multiplication. After that, the program requests for two numbers in response to which the user enters 40 and 58. The program at this point displays the equation done and the result.

Output
Please type in the math operation you would like to complete:
+ for addition
- for subtraction
* for multiplication
/ for division
*

Please enter the first number: 58
Please enter the second number: 40
58 * 40 =
2320

Because of the way the program is structured, when the user inputs % when asked for an operation at the initial prompt, he will not get any feedback to try again until after he enters numbers. You can try considering other possible options for handling different situations.

So far, you have a perfectly functional program. However, you cannot perform a second or third operation if you do not run the program once more–just go ahead and add a bit more functionality to your program.

Define the functions

Defining particular functions is important because it allows the program the capacity to perform the program multiple times as per the user's needs. You will first place your current code block into a function. You will call the function 'calculate()' and then include another later of indentation inside the function. To make sure the program runs, you will also call the function at the foot of your file.

calculator.py

```
# Define our function
def calculate():
    operation = input('''
Please type in the math operation you would like to complete:
+ for addition
- for subtraction
* for multiplication
/ for division
''')

    number_1 = int(input('Please enter the first number: '))
    number_2 = int(input('Please enter the second number: '))

    if operation == '+':
        print('{} + {} = '.format(number_1, number_2))
        print(number_1 + number_2)

    elif operation == '-':
        print('{} - {} = '.format(number_1, number_2))
        print(number_1 - number_2)

    elif operation == '*':
        print('{} * {} = '.format(number_1, number_2))
        print(number_1 * number_2)

    elif operation == '/':
        print('{} / {} = '.format(number_1, number_2))
        print(number_1 / number_2)

    else:
        print('You have not typed a valid operator, please run the program again.')

# Call calculate() outside of the function
calculate()
```

After that, you will build a second function comprising more conditional statements. You want to provide a choice (to the user) to decide if he wants to calculate once more or not in this code block. You can have this based of your calculator conditional statements—in this case though, you will just have a single 'elif', a single 'if' and also a single 'else' for handling of errors.

You will call the function 'again()' before adding it below the code block 'def calculate():'

calculator.py

```
...
# Define again() function to ask user if they want to use the calculator again
def again():

    # Take input from user
    calc_again = input('''
Do you want to calculate again?
Please type Y for YES or N for NO.
''')

    # If user types Y, run the calculate() function
    if calc_again == 'Y':
        calculate()

    # If user types N, say good-bye to the user and end the program
    elif calc_again == 'N':
        print('See you later.')

    # If user types another key, run the function again
    else:
        again()

# Call calculate() outside of the function

calculate()
```

Even though we have an error, i.e., with managing with the statement 'else' above, you could do a bit better to admit, for instance, a lower case y along with n on top of upper-case Y and N. Go ahead and add the 'str.upper():' string function to be able to do that.

calculator.py

```
...
def again():
    calc_again = input('''
Do you want to calculate again?
Please type Y for YES or N for NO.
```

```
""")

    # Accept 'y' or 'Y' by adding str.upper()
    if calc_again.upper() == 'Y':
        calculate()

    # Accept 'n' or 'N' by adding str.upper()
    elif calc_again.upper() == 'N':
        print('See you later.')

    else:
        again()
...
```

You should now be able to include the function 'again()' to the end of the function 'calculate()' to be able to trigger the code asking the user if he wants to continue or not.

calculator.py

```
def calculate():
    operation = input('''
Please type in the math operation you would like to complete:
+ for addition
- for subtraction
* for multiplication
/ for division
''')

    number_1 = int(input('Please enter the first number: '))
    number_2 = int(input('Please enter the second number: '))

    if operation == '+':
        print('{} + {} = '.format(number_1, number_2))
        print(number_1 + number_2)

    elif operation == '-':
        print('{} - {} = '.format(number_1, number_2))
        print(number_1 - number_2)

    elif operation == '*':
        print('{} * {} = '.format(number_1, number_2))
        print(number_1 * number_2)
```

PYTHON PROGRAMMING FOR BEGINNERS

```python
    elif operation == '/':
        print('{} / {} = '.format(number_1, number_2))
        print(number_1 / number_2)

    else:
        print('You have not typed a valid operator, please run the program again.')

    # Add again() function to calculate() function
    again()

def again():
    calc_again = input('''
Do you want to calculate again?
Please type Y for YES or N for NO.
''')

    if calc_again.upper() == 'Y':
        calculate()
    elif calc_again.upper() == 'N':
        print('See you later.')
    else:
        again()
```

In your terminal window, you can now try running the program with 'python calculate.py' and you will have the ability to make any number of calculations you wish.

Improve the code:

CONGRATULATIONS! You now have a fully functional program!

Still, you can do much more to improve the code. For instance, you could add some 'welcome' function that welcomes folks into your program right at the top of the code like so:

```python
def welcome():
    print('''
Welcome to Calculator
''')
...
# Don't forget to call the function
welcome()

calculate()
```

You can also introduce many more error-handling all through the program. To begin with, you can make sure the program keeps running even if the person using the program enters 'plankton' instead of a number. As the program is now, if number_1 and number_2 are not recognizable integers, the user will simply receive an error and the program will not run.

Likewise, in cases where the user chooses the division operator and then enters zero for the second number, the user simply receives an error: 'ZeroDivisionError:division by zero. ' In this case, you will need to use exception handling with the statement 'try...except'.

Note that we only limited the program to four operations. You can add as many more operators as you want.

```
...
    operation = input('''
Please type in the math operation you would like to complete:
+ for addition
- for subtraction
* for multiplication
/ for division
** for power
% for modulo
''')
...
```

Don't forget to add more conditional statements to solve for power and modulo

Moreover, you may need to write a section of the program again using a loop statement. There are numerous ways to manage errors and improve or modify every coding project. It is vital to remember that there is no given or specific right way to solve a problem presented to you.

Conclusion

We have come to the end of the book. Thank you for reading and congratulations for reading until the end.

I truly hope that this book has helped you to master some basics of python programming language.

Python programming is fun, simple, and very straightforward, something you can now attest to.

We have covered a few important topics for an average beginner including:

1. Downloading and installing the program

2. Different ways of interacting with Python

3. How to begin: writing your first simple program

4. Learning methods and functions

5. Mastering Loops

6. Learning user-defined functions and

7. Examples of beginner Python programming projects

Those are seven topics, for seven days, one topic per day–if you are the lazy type. In other words, all factors considered, you can learn what we have discussed in this book in less than seven days and then advance to the next level: book 2 of Python programming.

If corporate executives from big tech companies like Google only have positives to say about python, you have no reason not to learn it with gusto.

"Python has been an important part of Google since the beginning, and remains so as the system grows and evolves. Today dozens of Google engineers use Python, and we're looking for more people with skills in this language."

If you found the book valuable, can you recommend it to others? One way to do that is to post a review on Amazon.

Click here to leave a review for this book on Amazon!

Python Programming
For Intermediates

Learn The Basics of Python in 7 Days

Maurice J. Thompson

information is without contract or any type of guarantee assurance.

The trademarks that are used are without any consent, and the publication of the trademark is without permission or backing by the trademark owner. All trademarks and brands within this book are for clarifying purposes only and are the owned by the owners themselves, not affiliated with this document.

Table of Contents

Introduction

I want to thank you and congratulate you for buying the book, *"Python Programming For Intermediates: Learn The Basics of Python in 7 Days"*.

This book is the ultimate guide to python programming for intermediates. It will enable you to learn all that in as little as 7 days.

Congratulations for making it to this level and welcome to the second edition of our Python programming in 7 days series. I hope you had fun with the beginner's edition and are ready to learn some more!

In case you have forgotten, Python is the best programming language for learners or established programmers not only because of its convenience and ease of use, but also because it makes coding so attractive and fun.

In this second edition of the tutorial, we will cover a range of topics that will help you understand and perform complex Python programming projects. My assumption is that you already know the basics of Python including downloading and installing important Python programs and working with the basic Python functions. Otherwise, you need to revisit the first edition to make sure you are ready to take on intermediate level programming.

Let us start by mentioning what we covered in the first edition of this series:

✓ Downloading and installing Python on major operating systems

✓ How to interact with Python

- ✓ Writing your first program

- ✓ Methods and functions–including variables, strings, lists, tuples, and dictionaries

- ✓ Loops

- ✓ User defined functions

- ✓ Beginner level Python projects

In this book, we will talk about the following:

- ✓ Shallow copy and deep copy

- ✓ Objects and classes in Python–including python inheritance, multiple inheritance, and so on

- ✓ Recursion in Python

- ✓ Debugging and testing

- ✓ Fibonacci sequence (definition) and Memoization in Python in Python

- ✓ Arguments in Python

- ✓ Namespaces in Python and Python Modules

- ✓ Simple Python projects for Intermediates

By reading this book, you will learn all that and much more. Let's begin.

Thanks again for downloading this book. I hope you enjoy it!

To start us off today, we will first talk about shallow and deep copy.

Shallow Copy, Deep Copy

From what you already know about Data Types and Variables, you know that Python is different from most other programming languages especially during the copying and assigning of simple data types such as strings and integers. The difference between deep copying and shallow copying is especially visible with compound objects, the objects that contain other objects such as class instances and lists.

The code snippet below shows Y pointing to the same memory location compared to X. This changes when a dissimilar value to Y is assigned. In our case here, if you still remember what we had learnt on data types and variables, y will get a separate memory location.

```
>>> x = 3
```

```
>>> y = x
```

However, even when this internal behavior appears strange compared to other languages such as C, Perl, and C++, the observable assignment results will answer your expectations. It can however be quite problematic if you copy mutable objects such as dictionaries and lists.

Python only builds real copies if it has to i.e. if the programmer, the user, demands it explicitly.

You will become acquainted with the most critical problems that can happen when you are copying different mutable objects i.e. whenever you are copying dictionaries and lists.

Let us look at copying a list.

```
>>> colours1 = ["red", "green"]
>>> colours2 = colours1
>>> colours2 = ["rouge", "vert"]
>>> print colours1
['red', 'green']
```

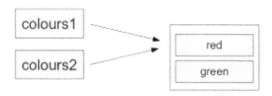

The above example shows a simple list being assigned to colors1. The subsequent step will entail assigning color1 to colors2. After this, a new list becomes assigned to colors2. As expected, the values of colors 1 do not change and as you may already know, a fresh memory location had been allotted for colors2 since we have assigned a full fresh list to this variable.

```
>>> colours1 = ["red", "green"]
>>> colours2 = colours1
>>> colours2[1] = "blue"
>>> colours1
['red', 'blue']
```

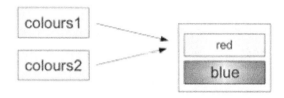

The question, nonetheless, is about what would happen when you changed an element of the colors2 and colors1 list. In the above example, a new value is assigned to the second element of colors2. Many beginners will be surprised to know that the colors1 list has also been changed 'automatically'. You can only explain this by saying that there have not been any new assignments to colors2 apart from one of its elements.

Using the Slice Operator

You can completely shallow copy the list structures using the slice operator without experiencing any of the side effects illustrated above:

```
>>> list1 = ['a','b','c','d']
>>> list2 = list1[:]
>>> list2[1] = 'x'
>>> print list2
['a', 'x', 'c', 'd']
>>> print list1
['a', 'b', 'c', 'd']
>>>
```

However, as soon as the list has sublists, you experience the same challenge i.e. just pointers to sublists.

```
>>> lst1 = ['a','b',['ab','ba']]
>>> lst2 = lst1[:]
```

The following diagram depicts this behavior perfectly:

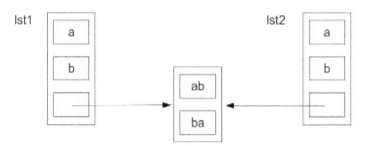

Assigning the 0th element a new value to of one of these lists ensures there are no side effects. When you tend to change a single element of the sublist, problems come up.

```
>>> lst1 = ['a','b',['ab','ba']]
>>> lst2 = lst1[:]
>>> lst2[0] = 'c'
>>> lst2[2][1] = 'd'
>>> print(lst1)
['a', 'b', ['ab', 'd']]
```

The diagram below shows what would happen if a single element of a sublist changes: the lst1 and lst2 contents are both changed.

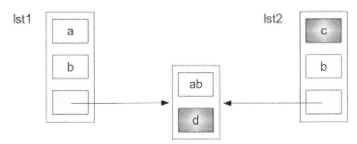

Using The Module's *Copydeep* Copy Method

A good way to approach the problems we have described is using the module *copy*. This module gives the 'copy' method, which in turn enables a total copy of an arbitrary list- that is, shallow, and the other lists.

Look at the example script below that uses the example above and the method here:

```
from copy import deepcopy

lst1 = ['a','b',['ab','ba']]

lst2 = deepcopy(lst1)

lst2[2][1] = "d"
lst2[0] = "c";

print lst2
print lst1
```

If you save our script and name it deep_copy.py, and if you call your script with 'python deep_copy.py', you will get the output below:

```
$ python deep_copy.py
['c', 'b', ['ab', 'd']]
['a', 'b', ['ab', 'ba']]
```

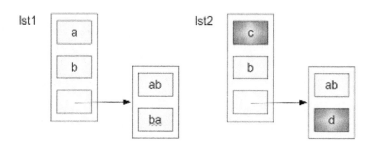

Recursion in Python (Recursive Functions)

Recursive is an adjective originating from 'recurrere', a Latin verb that means 'running back'. This is what a recursive function or a recursive definition does: it is simply returning to itself or "running back." If you have done some math, read something about programming, or even done computer science, you must have come across the factorial whose definition can be defined in arithmetic terms as follows:

n! = n * (n-1)!, if n > 1 and f(1) = 1

Meaning of Recursion

Recursion is a technique of coding or programming a problem where a function is calling itself once or many times in its body. Typically, it is taking back this function call's return value. When a function definition is fulfilling the recursion condition, you can refer to this function a recursive function.

In summary, a recursive function in Python is one that calls itself.

So far, you have seen numerous functions in Python that call other functions. Nonetheless, as the simple example below depicts, it is very possible for functions to call themselves:

```
# Program by Mitchell Aikens
# No Copyright
# 2010

num = 0
```

```
def main():
  counter(num)

def counter(num):
  print(num)
  num += 1
  counter(num)

main()
```

If you run the program in IDLE, it would do so endlessly. Only by stopping the loop by pressing Ctrl + C on the keyboard would you be able to interrupt the execution. This is a simple example of infinite recursion. A section of users have actually reported experiencing glitches in their IDLE systems bringing about the exception that is raised by Ctrl + C to begin looping as well. Whenever that occurs, you can press Ctrl+F6 for the IDLE shell to restart.

Arguably, recursion is another way of accomplishing the same result as a while loop. In some cases, this is completely correct. However, we have other recursion uses that are very valid where the 'for' and 'while' loops may not be ideal.

Just like loops, you need to note that recursion can be controlled. The example below depicts a controlled loop.

```
# Program by Mitchell Aikens
# No copyright
# 2012
def main():
  loopnum = int(input("How many times would you like to
loop?\n"))
  counter = 1
  recurr(loopnum,counter)
```

```
def recurr(loopnum,counter):
    if loopnum > 0:
        print("This is loop iteration",counter)
        recurr(loopnum - 1,counter + 1)
    else:
        print("The loop is complete.")

main()
```

The example above is using parameters or arguments to control the amount of recursions. Just use what you already know about functions and then follow the program flow.

Where can you apply recursion practically? Read the little section below that discuss a bit about the applications of this function.

Applications of Recursion

Usually, recursion is a computer science subject studied at an advanced level. The main use of recursion is to solve difficult or complex problems that one can break down into smaller, identical problems.

You do not entirely require recursion to solve a problem because many problems that recursion can solve can equally be solved using loops. Moreover, compared to a recursive function, a loop could be more efficient. Recursive functions typically need more resources and memory than loops, which makes them less efficient in many cases. At times, this usage requisite is called 'overhead'.

Having said that, I know you might now be asking yourself, "why waste time with recursion when I can just use a loop?" In any case, you already know how to use loops and this seems like pile of work. If you think so, I would totally understand even though it is ideal in itself. When you are trying to solve complex problems, a recursive function is a quicker, easier, and simpler way to construct and code.

You can think of the following 'rules':

- ✓ If you can solve the problem without recursion right now, the function just returns a value.

- ✓ If you cannot solve the problem without recursion now, the function cuts the problem into something smaller but similar, and then calls itself to be able to solve the problem.

We will use a common arithmetic concept I mentioned earlier to apply this: factorials.

A number 'n' has it's factorial represented by n!.

Look at the following fundamental rules of factorials.

n! = 1 if n = 0, and n! =1 x 2 x 3 x...x n if n > 0

For instance, the factorial of number 9 is as follows:

9! = 1 x 2 x 3 x 4 x 5 x 6 x 7 x 8 x 9

Below is a program that calculates any number's factorial that you, the user, keys in through the recursion technique.

```
def main():
    num = int(input("Please enter a non-negative integer.\n"))
    fact = factorial(num)
    print("The factorial of",num,"is",fact)

def factorial(num):
    if num == 0:
        return 1
    else:
        return num * factorial(num - 1)

main()
```

There is a topic that recursion is also useful in generators. We would require the code to generate the series 1,2,1,3,1,2,1,4,1,2...

```
def crazy(min_):
    yield min_
    g=crazy(min_+1)
    while True:
        yield next(g)
        yield min_

i=crazy(1)
```

You would then call next (i) to get the subsequent element.

Classes and Objects: Understanding their Meaning

As mentioned in the first edition, Python is an object oriented programming language. Thus, unlike the procedure-oriented programming that stresses functions, it emphasizes objects.

Simply put, objects are collection of data or variables and functions or methods acting on this data. On the other hand, a class acts as a blueprint for the object.

The class is just like a prototype or sketch of a house that contains all details about the doors, windows, floors, and so on. According to these descriptions, you build a house; the house is the object.

Since many houses can be built from a single description, you can make many objects from one class. An object can also be referred to as an instance of a class; the whole process of making this object is known as instantiation.

Defining a Class

Let us try Defining a class:

If you can remember correctly, in Python, functions begin with the 'def' keyword. On the other hand, the class is defined using the 'class' keyword. The first string is known as the docstring and contains a short description of the class. Even though not compulsory, it is recommended.

Look at the following simple definition of a class:

```
class MyNewClass:
    '''This is a docstring. I have created a new class'''
    pass
```

A class makes a fresh local namespace in which all the attributes have been defined. The attributes could be functions or data.

We also have special attributes contained in it starting with '__' (double underscores). For instance, _doc_ will give you the docstring of that particular class. There also exists different special attributes, which usually start with double underscores (__). A good example is __doc__, which gives us the docstring of that particular class.

When you define a class, it immediately creates a new class object that has the same name. Such a class object enables you to access the various attributes and then instantiate brand new objects of that particular class.

```
class MyClass:
    "This is my second class"
    a = 10
    def func(self):
        print('Hello')

# Output: 10
print(MyClass.a)

# Output: <function MyClass.func at 0x0000000003079BF8>
print(MyClass.func)

# Output: 'This is my second class'
print(MyClass.__doc__)
```

Running the program will give the following output:

```
10
<function 0x7feaa932eae8="" at="" myclass.func="">
This is my second class
```

Let us now create an object:

As you saw, you can use class object to gain access to various attributes. Well, you can also use it to make new instances of objects (instantiation) of the class. The process of creating an object is no different from that of creating a function call.

>>> ob = MyClass()

With that, you will have a new instance object named 'ob' created. You can access objects' attributes with the object name prefix.

Attributes may be method or data. The object methods are the conforming functions belonging to that class. Any function object recognized as a class attribute defines or describes a method for objects of that particular class. This simply means that because of the fact that 'MyClass.func' is a function object or class attribute, 'ob.func' will thus be a method object.

You must have noticed the parameter 'self' in the function definition within the class but we just called the method 'ob.func()' excluding any arguments and it still worked! The reason is simple; anytime objects call their methods, the objects themselves pass as the initial arguments. Thus 'on.func()' will end up translating to 'MyClass.func(ob)'.

Generally, when you call a method containing a list of arguments, you will realize that it is still the same as calling the corresponding or conforming function with a list of arguments made by putting in the method's object before the initial argument. Because of this, the initial function's argument in class has to be the object itself. Conventionally, this is known as 'self' and can be named differently (I would, however, really recommend you follow the convention).

At this point, you should be a pro at instance object, class object, method object, function object, and what differentiates them from each other.

Constructors

In classes, special functions are class functions starting with double underscores; we refer to them as special functions because they carry a special meaning.

One that should strike your interest is the function '__init__ ()'. This is a special function is usually called each time a new object of that class becomes instantiated. In object-oriented programming, this function type is called a constructor; it is normally used to initialize the whole list of variables.

```
class ComplexNumber:

  def __init__(self,r = 0,i = 0):

    self.real = r

    self.imag = i

  def getData(self):

    print("{0}+{1}j".format(self.real,self.imag))

# Create a new ComplexNumber object

c1 = ComplexNumber(2,3)

# Call getData() function

# Output: 2+3j
```

```
c1.getData()

# Create another ComplexNumber object

# and create a new attribute 'attr'

c2 = ComplexNumber(5)

c2.attr = 10

# Output: (5, 0, 10)

print((c2.real, c2.imag, c2.attr))

# but c1 object doesn't have attribute 'attr'

# AttributeError: 'ComplexNumber' object has no attribute 'attr'

c1.attr
```

The example above shows that you define a new class to stand in for the complex numbers. It contains two functions, which include __init__ () for the initializing of the variables (this defaults to zero) as well as 'getData ()' for the proper display of the number.

Something interesting you ought to note in the step above is that you can create the object's attributes as you go. For the object 'c2', a new attribute 'attr' was created and read. However, this did not make that attribute for the 'cl' object.

Deleting Attributes and Objects

You can delete any attribute of an object anytime with the del statement. To do so, try doing the following on the Python shell to get the output.

```
>>> c1 = ComplexNumber(2,3)
>>> del c1.imag
>>> c1.getData()
Traceback (most recent call last):
...
AttributeError: 'ComplexNumber' object has no attribute 'imag'

>>> del ComplexNumber.getData
>>> c1.getData()
Traceback (most recent call last):
...
AttributeError: 'ComplexNumber' object has no attribute
'getData'
```

You can actually delete the object itself with the 'del' statement.

```
>>> c1 = ComplexNumber(1,3)
>>> del c1
>>> c1
Traceback (most recent call last):
...
NameError: name 'c1' is not defined
```

It is actually a lot more complicated that just that. When you do 'c1 = ComplexNumber (1,3)' you will get a fresh instance object built in memory and the 'c1' name combines with it.

On the 'del c1', this attachment is removed and the 'c1' name is removed from the corresponding namespace. The object, nonetheless, continues existing in memory and if there is no other name bound to it, is later destroyed automatically. This destruction of unreferenced Python objects is also known as garbage collection.

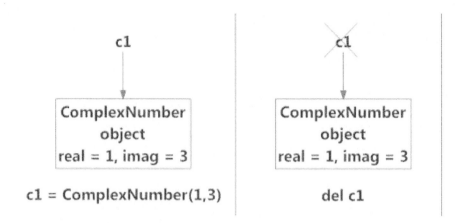

As you may already know, object-oriented programming builds reusable code patterns to restrain cases of redundancy in development projects. A good way object-oriented programming can achieve recyclable code is through inheritance, which is when one subclass leverages code from a different base class.

To learn more, we will go over some of the important aspects of inheritance in Python programming including learning the workings of child classes and parent classes, how you can override the attributes and methods, usage of the super() function, and how to use multiple inheritance.

Inheritance in Python

Inheritance is simply when a class uses code built within another class. You can look at inheritance in a biological manner: it is similar to a child inheriting particular traits from a parent. This means that the child can inherit the finger shape or color of the parent. At the same time, children can also share the last name with their parents.

Classes known as subclasses or child classes inherit variables and methods from base classes or parent classes. In this regard, think of the parent class known as 'parent' having class variables for 'finger shape', 'color' and 'height' the child class known as 'child' will inherit from its 'parent'.

Since the subclass 'child' inherits from the base class 'parent', the 'child' class can be able to reuse the code of 'parent', which then allows the programmer use less lines of code and reduce redundancy.

Parent Classes

Also called base classes, parent classes build a pattern out of which subclasses or child classes can be based on. The parent classes will allow you to construct child classes through inheritance without the need to write the same code repeatedly each time. Well, a class can become a parent class, and thus, they are each very functional or practical classes in their own right instead of mere templates.

As an example, we have, say, a general parent class: 'Bank_account' that contains the child classes: 'Business_account' and 'Personal_account'. Many of the methods between business accounts and personal accounts will be the same—like the methods to deposit and withdraw cash—thus, these can fit in the 'Bank_account' parent class. The subclass 'Business_account' would contain methods very specific to it, which may include a way of collecting business records and forms and as the variable 'employee_identification_number'.

In the same way, a class 'Animal' may contain methods like 'eating()'and 'sleeping()' just as a subclass 'Snake' could include its own methods like 'hissing()' and 'slithering()'.

Let us create a parent class 'fish' that we will later use to build the different types of fish to be its subclasses. Besides the characteristics, every one of these fishes will have first names and last names.

In this regard, you will create a file named 'fish.py' and begin with the '__init__() constructor method. You will populate it with the class variables: 'first_name' and 'last_name' for every subclass or 'fish' object.

fish.py

```
class Fish:
  def __init__(self, first_name, last_name="Fish"):
    self.first_name = first_name
    self.last_name = last_name
```

You have initialized your variable: 'last_name' with the 'Fish' string since you know that most fish will have that as their last name.

Let us now try adding other methods:

fish.py

```
class Fish:
  def __init__(self, first_name, last_name="Fish"):
    self.first_name = first_name
    self.last_name = last_name

  def swim(self):
    print("The fish is swimming.")

  def swim_backwards(self):
    print("The fish can swim backwards.")
```

As you can see, the 'swim()' and 'swim_backwards()' methods have been added to the 'fish class'; this will enable each subclass be able to use these methods.

Because most of the fish you will be creating are perceived as bony fish (meaning they have a bone skeleton) as opposed to the ones that contain a cartilage skeleton known as cartilaginous fish, you can include to the method '__init__()' a couple more attributes as follows:

fish.py

```
class Fish:
  def __init__(self, first_name, last_name="Fish",
        skeleton="bone", eyelids=False):
    self.first_name = first_name
    self.last_name = last_name
    self.skeleton = skeleton
    self.eyelids = eyelids

  def swim(self):
    print("The fish is swimming.")

  def swim_backwards(self):
    print("The fish can swim backwards.")
```

Creating a parent class will follow a methodology similar to creating any other class—it is just that we are sort of thinking about the kind of methods the child classes will use once created.

Child Classes

Subclasses or child classes are classes that inherit from parent classes. This means that every child class will have the ability to take advantage of the parent class' methods and variables. For instance, a child class 'Goldfish' that belongs to the subclass of 'fish' class will have the chance to use the 'swim()' method that has been declared in 'fish' without necessarily having to declare it.

You can look at every child class as taking the role of a class of the parent class. This means if you have a child class that is referred to as 'Rhombus' and its parent class named 'Parallelogram', you can say that a 'Rhombus' is actually a 'Parallelogram' much like a 'Goldfish' is a 'fish'.

The first child class' line looks a bit different from the non-child classes since you have to ensure the parent class passes into the child class as a parameter as follows:

class Trout(Fish):

In this case, the class 'Trout' is a child of the class 'Fish'. This is obvious because the word 'Fish' is included in the parentheses.

When it comes to child classes, you can choose to add more methods, override the current parent methods, or just accept the default parent methods using the keyword 'pass' as done in the case below:

fish.py

```
...
class Trout(Fish):
    pass
```

You can now build an object 'Trout' without needing to make definitions of any extra methods.

fish.py

```
...
class Trout(Fish):
    pass

terry = Trout("Terry")
print(terry.first_name + " " + terry.last_name)
print(terry.skeleton)
print(terry.eyelids)
terry.swim()
terry.swim_backwards()
```

You have created an object 'Trout' called 'terry' that uses every one of the methods of the class 'fish' even though you did not define these methods in the child class 'trout'. You only had to pass the 'terry' value to the variable 'first_name' since all the other variables were all initialized.

When you run the program, you get the following output:

```
Output
Terry Fish
bone
False
The fish is swimming.
The fish can swim backwards.
```

Now we will build an additional child class that contains its own methods. You use the name 'Clownfish' for this class; its special method will allow it to coexist with sea anemone--

fish.py

```
...
class Clownfish(Fish):

    def live_with_anemone(self):
        print("The clownfish is coexisting with sea anemone.")
```

After that, you can try creating an object 'clownfish' to see how this will work.

fish.py

```
...
casey = Clownfish("Casey")
print(casey.first_name + " " + casey.last_name)
casey.swim()
casey.live_with_anemone()
```

Running the program will give the output below:

```
Output
Casey Fish
The fish is swimming.
The clownfish is coexisting with sea anemone.
```

According to the output, we see that the object 'clownfish' named 'casey' can use the 'fish' methods 'swim()' and '__init__()' and also its child class method named 'live_with_anemone()'.

If you try using the method 'live_with_anemone()' in an object 'Trout', you simply get the following error:

Output
terry.live_with_anemone()
AttributeError: 'Trout' object has no attribute
'live_with_anemone'

The reason behind this is that the 'live_with_anemone()'
method belongs to the child class 'clownfish' and not the
parent class 'fish'.

The child class inherits the parent class methods it belongs to
and thus, every child class can use these methods inside
programs.

Overriding Parent Methods

So far, we have looked at the 'Trout' child class that has used
the keyword 'pass' to inherit all the behaviors of 'fish' parent
class. We have also looked at the 'Clownfish' child class that
inherited all the behaviors of the parent class and built its own
unique method that is specific to the child class.

At times though, you will want to use some of the behaviors of
the parent class but not the entire list. When you change the
methods of the parent class, you essentially override them.

When you are creating the child and parent classes, you really
have to keep the design of the program in mind. This will allow
overriding not to produce unnecessary, redundant code.

You will now create a child class 'shark' of the parent class
'fish'. Since you built the class 'fish' with the idea of primarily
creating a bony fish, you will need to create adjustments for the
class 'shark' rather than a cartilaginous fish. When it comes to
program design, if you had more than a single non-bony fish,

you would probably want to create separate classes for every one of these two fish types.

Unlike bony fish, sharks have skeletons made out of cartilage rather than bone. Sharks also have eyelids and cannot swim backwards. By sinking though, the sharks can be able to maneuver themselves backwards.

In this light, we will be overriding the constructor method '__init__()' as well as the method 'swim_backwards'. You do not have to change the method swim() because sharks can swim because they are fish.

Look at the child class below:

fish.py

```
...
class Shark(Fish):
  def __init__(self, first_name, last_name="Shark",
        skeleton="cartilage", eyelids=True):
    self.first_name = first_name
    self.last_name = last_name
    self.skeleton = skeleton
    self.eyelids = eyelids

  def swim_backwards(self):
    print("The shark cannot swim backwards, but can sink
backwards.")
```

You have just overridden the parameters (which have been initialized) in the method '__init__()'. The variable 'last_name' is thus at the moment set equal to the 'shark' string, the variable 'skeleton' is set equal to the 'cartilage' string, and the variable 'eyelids' is set to the 'true' Boolean value. Every instance of the class is also able to override the parameters here.

The 'swim_backwards()' method is now printing a different string than is the case in the parent class 'Fish' because sharks cannot swim backwards like a bony fish. You can now build an child class 'Shark' instance, which will still be able to use the method 'swim()' of the parent class 'fish'

fish.py

```
...
sammy = Shark("Sammy")
print(sammy.first_name + " " + sammy.last_name)
sammy.swim()
sammy.swim_backwards()
print(sammy.eyelids)
print(sammy.skeleton)
```

Running this code will give you the output below:

```
Output
Sammy Shark
The fish is swimming.
The shark cannot swim backwards, but can sink backwards.
True
cartilage
```

The child class 'Shark' overrode the __init__() successfully; it also did so for the method 'swim_backwards()' of the parent class 'Fish', at the same time inheriting the parent class method 'swim()'.

In case we have a restricted total child class numbers that are unique than the rest, overriding the methods of parent class are bound to be useful.

The Function 'Super()'

The function 'super()' can help you gain some access to the inherited methods overridden in a class object. When you use this function, you are essentially calling a parent method into a child method to be able to use it. For instance, you may want to override a single parent method's aspect with a particular functionality, but then call the other original parent method to complete the method.

In a students' grading program, you may want to have a parent's class method 'weighted_grade' overridden to be able to have the original class functionality included. When you invoke the function 'super()' you can achieve this.

This function is usually used inside the method __init__() as this is where you will most likely require adding a bit of uniqueness to the child class and then finish the initialization from the parent. Let us try modifying the child class 'Trout' so that you see how this works.

Trout are naturally freshwater fish; thus, you will have to include the variable 'water' to the method '__init__()' and set it equal to the 'freshwater' string, but then maintain the other parent class' parameters and variables:

fish.py

```
...
class Trout(Fish):
  def __init__(self, water = "freshwater"):
    self.water = water
    super().__init__(self)
...
```

As you can see the __init__() method has been overridden in the child class 'trout' thus giving a different implementation of the __init__() that is already defined by the 'fish' parent class.

Within the 'trout' class' __init__() method, the 'fish' class' __init__() method has been invoked explicitly.

Since you have overridden the method, you do not need to pass 'first_name' in as a 'trout' parameter anymore, and if you passed in a parameter, you would instead have to reset 'freshwater'. You will thus call the variable in your object instance to initialize the 'first_name'

You can now invoke the initialized parent class variables and use the unique child variable as well. Try using in the 'trout' instance:

fish.py

```
...
terry = Trout()

# Initialize first name
terry.first_name = "Terry"

# Use parent __init__() through super()
print(terry.first_name + " " + terry.last_name)
print(terry.eyelids)

# Use child __init__() override
print(terry.water)

# Use parent swim() method
terry.swim()
Output
Terry Fish
False
freshwater
The fish is swimming.
```

According to the output, the 'terry' object in the child class 'trout' can use the __init__() variable 'water' that is child specific while at the same time being able to call the __init__() variable of 'last_name', 'eyelids' and first_name in the 'fish' parent.

Thus, the inbuilt super() function in Python enables you to make good use of the parent class methods even when overriding particular aspects in our child classes of these methods.

Multiple Inheritance

A class can inherit methods and attributes from multiple parent classes in what we call multiple inheritance. It has the ability to allow programs to decrease redundancy and introduces a particular level of complexness not to mention ambiguity—thus, you should do it with the entire program design in mind.

We will try to make a child class 'coral_reef' that inherits from a 'sea_anemone' and 'coral' classes. You can create a method in each and use the keyword 'pass' in the child class 'coral_reef' as follows:

coral_reef.py

```
class Coral:

    def community(self):
        print("Coral lives in a community.")


class Anemone:

    def protect_clownfish(self):
        print("The anemone is protecting the clownfish.")


class CoralReef(Coral, Anemone):
    pass
```

The class 'coral' contains a method known as 'community()' that prints a single line, and the class 'anemone' contains a method known as 'protect_clownfish()' that prints another line. We then call both of these classes into the tuple inheritance. Therefore, 'coral' is simply inheriting from 2 parent classes.

We will now instantiate an object 'coral' as follows:

coral_reef.py

```
...
great_barrier = CoralReef()
great_barrier.community()
great_barrier.protect_clownfish()
```

The 'great_barrier' object has been created as a 'coralReef' object and can actually use the methods in the two parent classes. Running the program will give you the output below:

```
Output
Coral lives in a community.
The anemone is protecting the clownfish.
```

As you can see in the output, the methods from the two parent classes were effectively used in the child classes.

Multiple inheritances will allow you to use the code from multiple parent classes in a child class. If a similar method has been defined in more than one parent method, the child class then uses the method of the initial parent declared within its list of tuples.

While you can use multiple inheritances effectively, you need to do so with a lot of care so that the programs don't end up becoming ambiguous and hard for the other programmers to make out.

Operator Overloading

The different operators in Python work for in-built classes. When it comes to different types, the same operator behaves differently. For instance, the operator '+' performs addition (arithmetically) on two numbers, concatenates two strings, and merges two lists. This Python feature, a feature that gives the same operator the ability to have different meanings depending on the context, is known as operator overloading.

What would happen when you used them with user-defined class objects? Consider the class below that is trying to bring about a 2-D coordinate system simulation.

```
class Point:
    def __init__(self, x = 0, y = 0):
        self.x = x
        self.y = y
```

You can now try running the code and adding two points in the shell.

```
>>> p1 = Point(2,3)
>>> p2 = Point(-1,2)
>>> p1 + p2
Traceback (most recent call last):
...
TypeError: unsupported operand type(s) for +: 'Point' and 'Point'
```

As you can see, there are a whole lot of complains. The 'TypeError' came up because the program does not know how to combine two 'point' objects. Nonetheless, the good news is that with operator overloading, you can teach this to Python. First, however, we have to get an idea about special functions.

Python's Special Functions

Class functions that start with a double underscore are known as special functions. They, thus, are not ordinary. One of these functions is '__init__()' which you know very well. Each time you create a new object of that particular class, it gets called.

When you use the special functions, the class is made compatible with the in-built functions.

```
>>> p1 = Point(2,3)
>>> print(p1)
<__main__.Point object at 0x000000000031F8CC0>
```

This one did not print well but when you define the method '__str__()' in your class, you can control the way it gets printed. Thus, try adding this to your class.

```
class Point:
    def __init__(self, x = 0, y = 0):
        self.x = x
        self.y = y

    def __str__(self):
        return "({0},{1})".format(self.x,self.y)
```

We will now try the function 'print' once more.

```
>>> p1 = Point(2,3)
>>> print(p1)
(2,3)
```

You can see that what we get is better. In fact, this method is also used when we are using the built-in function 'format()' or 'str()'.

171

```
>>> str(p1)
'(2,3)'

>>> format(p1)
'(2,3)'
```

Thus, when you do 'format(p1)' or 'str(p1)', the program is doing p1.__str__(). Thus, the term special functions. That said, let us go back to operator overloading.

Overloading the Operator '+' In Python

To be able to overload the sign '+' you need to implement '__add__()' function in the class. You can do anything you want within this function. It is, nonetheless, only sensible to return the coordinate sum point object.

```
class Point:
    def __init__(self, x = 0, y = 0):
        self.x = x
        self.y = y

    def __str__(self):
        return "({0},{1})".format(self.x,self.y)

    def __add__(self,other):
        x = self.x + other.x
        y = self.y + other.y
        return Point(x,y)
```

Go ahead and try the addition once more.

```
>>> p1 = Point(2,3)
>>> p2 = Point(-1,2)
>>> print(p1 + p2)
(1,5)
```

What happens is that when we conduct p1+p2, the Python program calls p1.__add__(p2. This is in turn Point.__add__(p1,p2). Likewise, you can also overload the other operators. The special function needed to implement is illustrated in the table below:

Operator	Expression	Internally
Addition	p1 + p2	p1.__add__(p2)
Subtraction	p1 - p2	p1.__sub__(p2)
Multiplication	p1 * p2	p1.__mul__(p2)
Power	p1 ** p2	p1.__pow__(p2)
Division	p1 / p2	p1.__truediv__(p2)
Floor Division	p1 // p2	p1.__floordiv__(p2)
Remainder (modulo)	p1 % p2	p1.__mod__(p2)
Bitwise Left Shift	p1 << p2	p1.__lshift__(p2)
Bitwise Right Shift	p1 >> p2	p1.__rshift__(p2)
Bitwise AND	p1 & p2	p1.__and__(p2)
Bitwise OR	p1 | p2	p1.__or__(p2)
Bitwise XOR	p1 ^ p2	p1.__xor__(p2)
Bitwise NOT	~p1	p1.__invert__()

Overloading Python's Comparison Operators

In Python, operator overloading is not limited to just the arithmetic operators. You can also overload comparison operators.

For instance, say you wanted to include the < less than symbol in the Point class. We can compare the points' magnitude from the origin and for this purpose, return the result. Look at how you can implement this:

```
class Point:
  def __init__(self, x = 0, y = 0):
    self.x = x
    self.y = y


  def __str__(self):
    return "({0},{1})".format(self.x,self.y)


  def __lt__(self,other):
    self_mag = (self.x ** 2) + (self.y ** 2)
    other_mag = (other.x ** 2) + (other.y ** 2)
    return self_mag < other_mag
```

You can try the following sample and see how it runs in the shell:

```
>>> Point(1,1) < Point(-2,-3)
True

>>> Point(1,1) < Point(0.5,-0.2)
False

>>> Point(1,1) < Point(1,1)
False
```

In the same way, the table below shows the various special functions that we have to incorporate in order to overload the other comparison operators:

Operator	Expression	Internally
Less than	p1 < p2	p1.__lt__(p2)
Less than or equal to	p1 <= p2	p1.__le__(p2)
Equal to	p1 == p2	p1.__eq__(p2)
Not equal to	p1 != p2	p1.__ne__(p2)
Greater than	p1 > p2	p1.__gt__(p2)
Greater than or equal to	p1 >= p2	p1.__ge__(p2)

Breather: Debugging and Testing

Before we continue, how can you know that your programs are working? Can you really count on yourself to write flawless code every time? That is highly unlikely. Without a doubt, it is simple to write code in Python most of the time, but there are chances that your code will have bugs.

For any programmer, debugging is a life fact that plays an integral role in the programming craft. The only way you can begin debugging is running your program—obviously. When you run your program, it might not be enough. For instance, if you have written a program that processes files in a way, you will need a couple of files to run it on. If you have conversely written a utility library using arithmetic functions, you will need to supply these functions with parameters to be able to get the code to run.

Programmers do this sort of thing every time. In the compiled languages, the cycle goes 'edit-compile-run' *or something like that* repeatedly. In some instances, even creating the program to run could be a problem and you, the programmer, thus has to switch between editing and compiling. The compilation step is not available in Python. You thus have to edit and run only. Running the program is what testing is all about.

First Run and Code After

Change and flexibility is important for your code to survive at least to the end of the process of development. To plan for it, you really have to set up tests for the different sections of your program—commonly referred to as 'unit tests'. This is also a highly pragmatic and practical part of designing your

176

application. Instead of trying to 'code a bit and test a bit', the intuitive, the extreme programming crowd has brought to us the very useful but quite counterintuitive maxim: 'test a bit and code a bit'.

In different terms, you test first and then code later—in what we also refer to as test-driven programming. This approach could seem unfamiliar at first but it has numerous advantages and over time, it grows on you. In the end, once you have used test-driven programming for a while, writing code without putting it into use could appear backwards.

Precise Requirement Specification

When you are developing software, you first need to know the kind of problem the software needs to solve and the objectives it needs to meet. You can write a requirement specification to clarify your goals for the program—this document could also be some quick notes that describe the requirements the program should meet. With that, it is easier to check if the requirements have been satisfied.

However, most programmers do not like writing reports and generally prefer having the computer doing as much of the work as possible. Well, the good news is that you can specify your requirements and use the interpreter to check whether they have been satisfied.

The idea here is to start with writing a test program and then writing a program that passes the tests. This test program is simply the requirement specification and helps you stick to the requirements as you develop the program.

In case you are lost, we will look at an easy example.

Supposing you need to write a module containing one function that will calculate the area of a rectangle—i.e. with a known width and height—before you begin to code. In this case, you start by writing a unit test with a couple of examples whose answers you already know. The test program could look something like the one below (listing 1).

The simple test program

```
from area import rect_area

height = 3

width = 4

correct_answer = 12

answer = rect_area(height, width)

if answer == correct_answer:
    print('Test passed ')
else:
    print('Test failed ')
```

The example above shows that we call the 'recta_area' function—not yet written—on the height and width (these are 3 and 4 respectively) and then compare the result with the right one, which in this case is 12.

If thereafter, you implement rect_area carelessly (in the file area.py) as described below and try running the test program, you will receive an error message.

```
def rect_area(height, width):

    return height * height # This is wrong ...
```

You could then try examining the code to see what the problem was and replacing the expression returned with height * width.

When you write a test before writing your code, you do not do so just as preparation for finding bugs; you do so as preparation for seeing if your code is working in the first place.

The question with your code therefore is, until you test the code, does it really do anything? You can use it to have the outlook that a feature does not really exist until you have found a test for it. This means you can clearly demonstrate that it is there and doing what it ought to do. This is definitely useful for you as you develop the program at first, as well as when you extend and maintain the code later on.

Plan for change

Apart from being greatly helpful as you write the program, the automated tests help you evade accumulated errors when you make changes. This is particularly important as your program grows in size. You have to be prepared to change your code instead of clinging to what you have: change comes with its dangers.

Changing a piece of code might often mean you have introduced an unexpected bug or more. If you make sure you have properly designed your program, this is with the right abstraction and encapsulation, the change effects should be local, and affect a little part of the code. If you therefore spot the bug, debugging becomes easier.

The testing '1-2-3'

Look at the following breakdown of the process of development that is essentially test-driven (this is a version of it at least). This is necessary before we get into the details of writing tests.

✓ Make out the new feature you need. Try documenting it and then writing a test for it.

✓ Write a skeleton code for this feature so that your program is running devoid of any syntax errors or things like that, but (note) so your test is still failing. You have to see your test fail so that you are sure that it in fact CAN fail. If you note a problem with the test and it is always succeeding regardless, it simply means you are not testing anything.

✓ Write a dummy code for the skeleton to appease the test. This does not have to implement the functionality accurately but simply make the tests pass. This in turn allows you to have all your tests passing all the time when you are developing (except the first time you try to run the test), even as you first implement the functionality.

✓ Refactor or rewrite the code so that it is actually doing what it ought to do, while at the same time trying to ensure your test is still succeeding.

You need to keep your code in a good state when you leave it; do not leave it with tests failing or in this case, succeeding with the dummy code still present.

Another thing; before we continue, we need to look at something important known as the Fibonacci sequence because you are sure to come across it sooner or later in this Python series—starting with the next chapter. We will cover it lightly and briefly so that you can continue without any hassle.

The Fibonacci sequence

The Fibonacci sequence is simply a group of numbers starting with a zero or one, followed by a one and goes on according to the rule that every number—known as a Fibonacci number—is equivalent to the sum of the two preceding numbers. If the Fibonacci sequence is symbolized F(n) in which n represents the first sequence term, the equation below obtains for n = 0 in which the first two terms are conventionally defined as 0 and 1.

$F (0) = 0, 1, 1, 2, 3, 5, 8, 13, 21, 34...$

You will find in some texts a custom of using n=1 in which case the definition of the first two terms is 1 and 1 — this is by default, and thus:

$F (1) = 1, 1, 2, 3, 5, 8, 13, 21, 34...$

The Fibonacci sequence draws its name from Fibonacci or Leonardo Pisano, a mathematician from Italy who lived from between 1170 and 1250. Fibonacci used the mathematical series to describe a problem according to two breeding rabbits.

He would thus ask, "how many pairs of rabbits would be produced per year, starting with one pair, if in each month, each one (pair) is bearing a fresh pair that becomes productive starting from the second month?" The numerical expression of the result is as follows: 1, 1, 2, 3, 5, 8, 13, 21, 34...

Physicists and biologists alike are usually interested in the Fibonacci numbers because they are present in different phenomena and natural objects. Branching leaves and trees patterns, for instance, and the distribution of raspberry seeds in a raspberry are all based on the Fibonacci numbers.

Lastly, you ought to know that the Fibonacci sequence has a relationship with the <u>golden ratio</u>. This is a proportion that is about 1:1.6 occurring a lot throughout the natural world and is practical in numerous areas of human effort. The golden ratio and Fibonacci sequence are used to guide architectural design and that for user interfaces and websites—among many other things.

Memoization in Python

Memoization is the method of caching a functional call's results. When you memoize a function, you can only evaluate it by looking up the result you obtained the first time you used those parameters to call the function. The log for this is in the Memoization cache. The lookup might fail—to mean the function failed to call with the parameters. Only then would running the function itself be necessary.

Memoization does not make sense unless the function is deterministic, or you can simply accept the result as out of date. However, if the function were expensive, a massive speedup would be the result of the memorization. Essentially, you are dealing the function's computational complexity for the lookup's complexity.

Let us take it back little.

As a programmer, you know recursion gives you a convenient way of breaking bigger problems into smaller, manageable pieces. Try considering iterative set against recursive solutions for a Fibonacci sum (even though we will talk more about Fibonacci in a bit).

```
# iterative
def fib_iterative(n):
    if (n == 0):
        return 0
    elif (n == 1):
        return 1
    elif (n >1):
        fn = 0
        fn1 = 1
        fn2 = 2
        for i in range(3, n):
```

```
            fn = fn1+fn2
            fn1 = fn2
            fn2 = fn
        return fn
# recursive
def fib(n):
    if n == 0: return 0
    if n == 1: return 1
    else: return fib(n-1) + fib(n-2)
```

Recursive solutions are usually simpler when reading and writing for the branching problems. You will notice that tree traversals, mathematical series, and graph traversals are usually—intuitively so—dealt with more using recursion. Even though it offers a lot of convenience, the recursion computational time cost on branching problems exponentially grows with bigger 'n' values.

Look at the fib (6) call stack below:

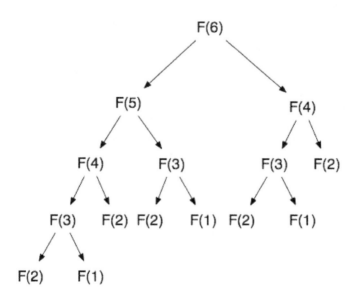

At each successive tree level, you perform twice as many operations and that gives you a time complexity: o (2^n)

184

If you take a better look at the tree, you will easily notice a repetition of the work. While fib(2) compute five times, the fib(3) computes three times and so forth. Even though this is not an issue for small 'n' values, consider the possible amount of repeated work in computing fib(1000). When you have revised your recursive solution, you can try to run the same problem—say fib of 20—for the two versions and see the remarkable time difference to completion.

There is a practical way of preventing repeated work and keeping your elegant solution.

The Fibonacci Square

The usual Memoization expository example is the Fibonacci sequence where every item in the sequence is the sum total of the previous double items. Look at a Python implementation below:

```
def fib(n):
  if n <= 2:
    return 1
  else:
        return fib(n - 2) + fib(n - 1)
```

The naïve recursive approach has a problem in that the total number of calls swells exponentially with n- that makes it quite expensive for the large n:

```
In [1]: [_ = fib(i) for i in range(1, 35)]
CPU times: user 30.6 s, sys: 395 ms, total: 31 s
    Wall time: 31.9 s
```

To make an evaluation of fib (10), you require to compute fib(8) as well as fib(9). However, we already computed the former when computing the latter. The trick here is remembering these results. This is what we know as Memoization.

This section has a mnemonic you can be able to memorize a function in the latest version of Python by importing 'functools' and also adding the decorator '@functools.lru_cache' to the function. We will discuss this towards the end of this section.

If you want to know a little more about the way memorization works in Python, and why doing it manually has ugly compromises (syntactically) and what decorators are, you can continue reading on the manual Memoization approaches.

Manual Memoization (Memoization by Hand)

The first Memoization approach involves taking advantage of an infamous Python feature: to add state to a function as follows:

```
def fib_default_memoized(n, cache={}):
  if n in cache:
    ans = cache[n]
  elif n <= 2:
    ans = 1
    cache[n] = ans
  else:
    ans = fib_default_memoized(n - 2) +
fib_default_memoized(n - 1)
    cache[n] = ans

    return ans
```

The basic logic ought to be very obvious: the 'cache' is a results dictionary of the earlier calls to 'fib_default_memoized()'. The 'n' parameter is the key; the nth Fibonacci number is the value. If it is that way, you are done, but if it is not, you have to evaluate it as in the version of the native recursive and keep it in the cache before the return of the result.

The thing here is 'cache' is the function's keyword parameter. Python usually evaluates the keyword parameters just once, which is upon importation of the function. This simply means that if there is mutability in the keyword parameter—note that a dictionary is—it therefore just gets initialized once. This is usually the basis of subtle bugs but in this case, you mutate the keyword parameter to take advantage of it. The changes made—that is populating the cache—do not become wiped out by the 'cache={}' in the function definition, since the expression does not become evaluated once more.

Memoization gets you a speedup of six magnitude orders from seconds to microseconds. That is very nice if you think about it.

```
In [2]: %time [_ = fib_default_memoized(i) for i in range(1, 35)]
CPU times: user 33 µs, sys: 0 ns, total: 33 µs
    Wall time: 37.9 µs
```

Manual Memoization: Objects

Some Python programmers argue that mutating the formal function parameters is not a good idea. For others—especially programmers who use Java—the argument is that functions with state should be turned into objects. Look at how that might look below:

```
class Fib():

  cache = {}

  def __call__(self, n):
    if n in self.cache:
      ans = self.cache[n]
    if n <= 2:
```

```
        ans = 1
        self.cache[n] = ans
    else:
        ans = self(n - 2) + self(n - 1)
        self.cache[n] = ans

        return ans
```

In this case, the __call__ dunder method is used to make 'Fib'
instances behave like functions (syntactically). 'Cache' is
shared by all 'Fib' instances because it is a class attribute.
When you are evaluating Fibonacci numbers, you will find this
very desirable. However, if the object made calls to a server
well defined in the constructor, and the result was depending
on the server, it would not be a good thing. You would then
move it into an object attribute by taking it right into
'__init__'. Notwithstanding, you receive the memoization
speedup:

In [3]: f = Fib()

In [4]: %time [_ = f(i) for i in range(1, 35)]
CPU times: user 116 μs, sys: 0 ns, total: 116 μs
    Wall time: 120 μs

Well, in 2012, Jack Diederich gave a great PyCon talk known as
'stop writing classes' (watch it here– make sure to watch all of
it). If I were to give you a snippet or the short version of it, I
would say that a python class that has only two methods and
one of them is __init__ has a foul code smell (read more).
Class Fib up it does not have two methods all the same.
Additionally, it is about four times slower when compared to
the hacky default parameter method primarily because of the
object lookup overhead. Well, it stinks.

Manual Memoization: Using 'Global'

You have the ability to evade the default parameters hacky mutations and the over-engineered object resembling Java, by just using 'global'. 'Global does get a bad blow but if you ask me, it is good enough (perhaps because <u>it's acceptable with Peter</u> Norvig).

I would personally prefer that the 'global here' declarations add a little less optical clutter than the 32 'self' instances required for the class definition. Our Fib class does not exactly contain 32 'self' instances but you can argue that you would find better readability in the global version.

```python
global_cache = {}

def fib_global_memoized(n):
  global global_cache
  if n in global_cache:
    ans = global_cache[n]
  elif n <= 2:
    ans = 1
    global_cache[n] = ans
  else:
    ans = fib_global_memoized(n - 2) + fib_global_memoized(n - 1)
    global_cache[n] = ans

    return ans
```

This is not different from the default hacky parameter method, but here, we make it global to make sure the 'cache' remains across the function calls.

The object, default parameter, and the global cache methods are all completely satisfactory. Nonetheless, the good news is that in Python, especially the most current version, the 'Iru_cache' decorator was put in place to solve the problem for us.

189

Decorators

A decorator is simply a function in the higher-order. This means it takes a function as its argument and returns another function. When it comes to decorators, the returned function is typically only the original function, which has been augmented with a bit of additional functionality. If I were to give the most basic case, I would say that the added functionality is what I would referred to as a pure clean side effect such as logging. As an example, we can make a decorator, which has the ability to print some text every time the function it is decorating is called as follows:

```
def output_decorator(f):
  def f_(f)
    f()
    print('Ran f...')
      return f_
```

You can take the decorated version to replace the f. Just do 'F=output_decorator(f)'. By now calling f(), you get the decorated version, i.e. the original function as well as the print output. Python makes this even simpler with a bit of syntactic sugar as follows:

```
@output_decorator
def f()
        # ... define f ...
```

If that did not make a lot of sense, you could try understanding decorators, a tutorial by Simeon Franklin that takes you right from the basics of first class functions all the way to the decoration principles in just twelve steps.

You will agree that our output_decorator's side effect is not very motivating. However, you can go beyond clean side effects and augment the function's operation itself. For instance, the decorator could include the sort of cache precisely needed for memoization and then intercept calls to the function that is decorated whenever the result is in the cache already.

However, if you try writing your own memoization decorator, you could get mired fast in the particulars of argument passing and get really stuck with the introspection of Python when you figure that out. Introspection is the capacity to determine, at runtime, the type of an object—it is one of the numerous strengths of Python Language.

In other words, decorating a function naively is a great way of breaking the features the code is dependent on (and the interpreter) to learn about the function. You can check out the 'decorator module' documentation. The 'wrap' and 'decorator' modules figure out these introspection matters for you if you are satisfied with using non-standard library code.

Luckily, the fiddly details of the decorator have been worked out for the specific memorization case; the solution is also within the standard library.

functools.lru_cache

If you are running the latest version of Python (or at least 3.2), the only thing you need to do to memoize a function is simply apply the decorator: functools.lru_cache as follows:

```python
import functools

@functools.lru_cache()
def fib_lru_cache(n):
    if n < 2:
        return n
    else:
        return fib_lru_cache(n - 2) + fib_lru_cache(n - 1)
```

As you can see, this is just the original function with a decorator as well as an additional 'import'. What could be simpler? Applying this decorator actually offers the six magnitude speedup orders, which is expected.

```
In [5]: %time [fib.fib_lru_cache(i) for i in range(1, 35)]
CPU times: user 57 µs, sys: 1 µs, total: 58 µs
      Wall time: 61 µs
```

In case you are wondering, the LRU that is in 'lru_cache' symbolizes least recently used. This is a FIFO approach to managing the cache's size that could grow very large for the functions that are more complicated than fib().

However, fundamentally, the method taken by the standard library decorator to memoization is very much like has been discussed above. Actually, we have this decorator's backports in case you find yourself stuck on Python 2.7 or just want a speedy peek at the code.

Lru_cache definitely has compromises as well as overheads (consider that fib_lru_cache takes half the speed of your initial memoization attempt). Nonetheless, its trivial decorator interface sort of makes it very easy to use so much that it can be as simple as throwing a switch when you get a good place in your app for memoization.

Arguments in Python

You can define functions in Python taking variable number of arguments. You can use keyword, or arbitrary and default arguments to define these functions. In this section, we will delve into that.

In the previous edition (beginner's book), we covered a lot on user-defined functions. Particularly, we learnt all about defining functions and calling them. The function call, otherwise, results into errors. Look at the example below:

```
def greet(name,msg):
    """This function greets to
    the person with the provided message"""
    print("Hello",name + ', ' + msg)


greet("Monica","Good morning!")
```

The output is as follows:

Hello Monica, Good morning!

The 'greet()' function here has two parameters.

Since you have called this function containing two arguments, it will run smoothly and you will not receive any error.

If you use different number of arguments, the interpreter only complains. Below is a call function containing a single and no arguments together with their individual error messages.

```
>>> greet("Monica")   # only one argument
TypeError: greet() missing 1 required positional argument: 'msg'
>>> greet()   # no arguments
    TypeError: greet() missing 2 required positional arguments:
    'name' and 'msg'
```

Variable Function Arguments

Up until now, functions contained a fixed number of arguments. Python has other ways of defining a function that can assume variable argument numbers. Described below are the three various types of this kind:

1: Python Default Arguments

In Python, function arguments can contain default values. We can use the assignment operator denoted as '=' to offer a default value to an argument. Look at the example below:

```
def greet(name, msg = "Good morning!"):
    """

    This function greets to

    the person with the

    provided message.


    If message is not provided,

    it defaults to "Good

    morning!"
    """
```

```
print("Hello",name + ', ' + msg)
```

```
greet("Kate")
greet("Bruce","How do you do?")
```

The parameter 'name' in this function does not contain a default value and during a call, it is compulsory. Conversely, the 'msg' parameter contains a default 'good morning!' value. Thus, during a call, it is optional. If a value is offered, it overwrites the default value.

In a function, any given number of arguments can contain a default value but when you have a default argument, all arguments to its right have to have default values as well. This thus means that there is no way non-default arguments can follow the default arguments. For instance, if we had the function header defined above as follows:

```
def greet(msg = "Good morning!", name):
```

In this case, you would receive the following error

```
SyntaxError: non-default argument follows default argument
```

2: Python Keyword Arguments

When you use some values to call a function, these values are assigned to the arguments based on their position. For instance, in the 'greet()' function above, the 'Bruce' value in "greet(Bruce, how do you do?")" becomes assigned to the 'name' argument and likewise "how do you do?" to 'msg'.

Python allows for the use of keyboard arguments to call functions. When you call functions in this way, the position or

195

order of the arguments can become altered—the Following calls to the function above are valid and give out the same result.

```
>>> # 2 keyword arguments
>>> greet(name = "Bruce",msg = "How do you do?")

>>> # 2 keyword arguments (out of order)
>>> greet(msg = "How do you do?",name = "Bruce")

>>> # 1 positional, 1 keyword argument
    >>> greet("Bruce",msg = "How do you do?")
```

You can see that we can combine keyword arguments with positional arguments in the course of a function call. We, however, consider the fact that keyword arguments must go with positional arguments.

When you have a positional argument following keyword arguments, it will give out errors— for instance, look at the function call below:

greet(name="Bruce","How do you do?")

This results into following error:

SyntaxError: non-keyword arg after keyword arg

3: Arbitrary Arguments in Python

At times, you will not know in advance the number of arguments to be passed into a function. Python lets you handle this sort of situation using function calls with arbitrary argument numbers.

In the function definition, you can use the asterisk symbol (*) before the name of the parameter to signify this type of argument. Take the example below:

```
def greet(*names):
    """This function greets all
    the person in the names tuple."""

    # names is a tuple with arguments
    for name in names:
        print("Hello",name)


greet("Monica","Luke","Steve","John")
```

The output is as follows:

```
Hello Monica
Hello Luke
Hello Steve
        Hello John
```

Here, we have called the function using multiple arguments. These arguments become wrapped into a tuple long before they are moved into the function. Within the function, the 'for loop' is used to recover all the arguments.

As you must have seen so far, Python functions have an extra variety of features that are bound to make the life of a Python programmer a lot simpler. While some of these are the same as the capabilities contained in different other programming languages, many of them are only available in Python. Such extras can actually make a purpose of a function a bit more obvious. For instance, they can get rid of noise and bring some clarity to the intention of callers. With these, the subtle bugs, which tend to be hard to find also reduce.

In the next section, we shall discuss the best practices when it comes to Python function arguments.

Best Practice for Python Function Arguments

When it comes to dealing with function arguments in Python, you should keep the following best practices in mind:

1: Using variable positional arguments to reduce visual noise

In reference to the parameter's conventional name, args*, optional positional arguments are also known as 'star args'. When you accept these optional positional arguments, you can make a function call clearer and eliminate 'visual noise'.

For instance, assume you want to log or record a bit of debug information. You would require a function taking a message and a group of values.

```
def log(message, values):
    if not values:
        print(message)
    else:
        values_str = ', '.join(str(x) for x in values)
        print('%s: %s' % (message, values_str))

log('My numbers are', [1, 2])
log('Hi there', [])

>>>
My numbers are: 1, 2
Hi there
```

When you have to pass an empty list without any values to log, it is burdensome and noisy. Entirely leaving out the second argument would be better. In Python, you can do this by simply prefixing the final positional parameter with the use of *. The

199

first log message parameter is needed—although whichever number of succeeding positional arguments are entirely optional. Save for the callers, the function body does not have to change.

```python
def log(message, *values):  # The only difference
    if not values:
        print(message)
    else:
        values_str = ', '.join(str(x) for x in values)
        print('%s: %s' % (message, values_str))

log('My numbers are', 1, 2)
log('Hi there')  # Much better

>>>
My numbers are: 1, 2
    Hi there
```

If you have a list ready and maybe desire to call a variable argument function such as 'log', you can simply use the * operator to achieve that. This will tell Python to pass the items as positional arguments from the sequence.

```python
favorites = [7, 33, 99]
log('Favorite colors', *favorites)

>>>
    Favorite colors: 7, 33, 99
```

When it comes to taking a variable number of positional arguments, we have two issues. For one, variable arguments are converted into tuples before being transferred to your function. What this means is that when your function's caller uses the asterisk operator within a generator, it is then iterated to its exhaustion. The tuple that results will include each value from the generator, which could use up a lot of memory, which would cause your program to crash.

```
def my_generator():
  for i in range(10):
    yield i

def my_func(*args):
  print(args)

it = my_generator()
my_func(*it)

>>>
    (0, 1, 2, 3, 4, 5, 6, 7, 8, 9)
```

The function that accept *args are normally the most ideal for those situations where the number of inputs in the list of arguments will be sensibly small. This is perfect for the function calls passing multiple literals or names of variables together. Primarily, it is for the convenience of the programmer and code readability.

The other problem with *args is that in future, you cannot add fresh positional arguments to the function without having to migrate each caller. When you try adding positional arguments before the argument list, the current callers will break (subtly) if not properly updated.

```
def log(sequence, message, *values):
  if not values:
    print('%s: %s' % (sequence, message))
  else:
    values_str = ', '.join(str(x) for x in values)
    print('%s: %s: %s' % (sequence, message, values_str))

log(1, 'Favorites', 7, 33)    # New usage is OK
log('Favorite numbers', 7, 33) # Old usage breaks

>>>
1: Favorites: 7, 33
    Favorite numbers: 7: 33
```

The next call to 'log' in this case used 7 as the parameter 'message' since an argument 'sequence' was not provided—therefore, this is the problem here. Such kinds of bugs are usually difficult to track down because the code is still running and not raising any exceptions as it does so. You can use keyword-only arguments if you want to avoid this possibility completely—use them when you need to extend function accepting *args.

Even though some of them might appear overemphasized, please remember the following things:

✓ Functions accept positional argument variable numbers with the use of *args within the def statement.

✓ The items that are in the sequence can be used as positional arguments for functions using the *operator.

✓ When you use the * operator along with a generator, you might deplete your program's memory and lead to its eventual crash.

✓ Some coding bugs are difficult to find; in most cases, the introduction of these bugs happens when you add to the function fresh positional parameters that accept *args.

2: Offer Optional Behavior Using Keyword Arguments

Like current programming languages, calling a Python function makes it possible to pass arguments by position.

```python
def remainder(number, divisor):
    return number % divisor

    assert remainder(20, 7) == 6
```

You can also pass the entire list of positional arguments to the functions by a keyword; in this case, we use the argument's name in an assignment inside the function call parentheses. The arguments of the keyword can actually be passed in whichever order provided the needed positional arguments are well specified. You can combine and match positional arguments and keyword arguments. The calls are the same:

```
remainder(20, 7)
remainder(20, divisor=7)
remainder(number=20, divisor=7)
    remainder(divisor=7, number=20)
```

You need to specify positional arguments before the keyword arguments.

```
remainder(number=20, 7)
```

```
>>>
```
SyntaxError: non-keyword arg after keyword arg

Each argument can only be specified once.

```
remainder(20, number=7)
```

```
>>>
```
TypeError: remainder() got multiple values for argument 'number'

3: The keyword arguments' flexibility gives three major benefits

First, keyword arguments offer more clarity to the function call, which benefits new readers of the code. With regards to the 'remainder(20,7)' call, it is not crystal clear which argument represents the number and which one represents the divisor without looking at the 'remainder' method implementation. In the keyword arguments call, the 'divisor=7' and 'number=20' make it obvious, almost immediately, the kind of parameter in use for every purpose.

Secondly, the keyword arguments have a special impact: by default, they can have values specified in the function definition. This lets a function offer extra capabilities when you require them, but most of the time, also allows you to accept the default behavior. This may come in handy in getting rid of the repetitive code and reducing noise.

For instance, assume you want to calculate the rate of a certain fluid flowing into a vat. If in this case the vat is on a scale as well, you could use the two weight measurements' difference at two different times to know the rate of flow.

```
def flow_rate(weight_diff, time_diff):
    return weight_diff / time_diff

weight_diff = 0.5
time_diff = 3
flow = flow_rate(weight_diff, time_diff)
print('%.3f kg per second' % flow)

>>>
        0.167 kg per second
```

It is important to know, in the typical case, the rate of flow in kg's per second. At other times, it would be great to use the final sensor measurements to make approximations of bigger time scales such as hours or days. You can also add an argument for the scaling factor in the time period to offer the behavior in the same function.

```
def flow_rate(weight_diff, time_diff, period):
        return (weight_diff / time_diff) * period
```

Well, the issue is that now you have to specify the argument 'period' each time you call the function; this includes the common case of the rate of flow per seconds where the period is 1.

```
flow_per_second = flow_rate(weight_diff, time_diff, 1)
```

To make this a bit less noisy, you can offer the argument 'period' a default value.

```
def flow_rate(weight_diff, time_diff, period=1):
    return (weight_diff / time_diff) * period
```

4: The argument 'period' is now optional

```
flow_per_second = flow_rate(weight_diff, time_diff)
    flow_per_hour = flow_rate(weight_diff, time_diff,
    period=3600)
```

This works perfectly for the simple default values but you need to note that it gets a bit tricky for the complex default values. Look at the next subtopic talking about using 'none' and docstrings to specify the dynamic default arguments up next.

The other reason why you need to use keyword arguments is that they offer a great way of extending the parameters of a function while remaining backwards compatible with the prevailing callers. This allows you to offer extra functionality without necessarily having to move a load of code, which in turn lessens the chance of buggy code.

As an example, assume you need to extend the above function 'flow_rate' to compute the rate of flows in weight units alongside kilograms. You can achieve this by adding fresh optional parameters that offer a conversion rate to your chosen units of measurement.

```
def flow_rate(weight_diff, time_diff,
      period=1, units_per_kg=1):
    return ((weight_diff * units_per_kg) / time_diff) * period
```

The 'units_per_kg' has a default argument value of 1, making the returned weight units stay as kilograms. This means no existing callers shall see a behavioral change. New callers to the 'flow_rate' can then specify the fresh keyword argument to observe the fresh behavior.

```
pounds_per_hour = flow_rate(weight_diff, time_diff,
                  period=3600, units_per_kg=2.2)
```

The only issue with this kind of approach is that the optional keyword arguments such as 'units_per_kg' and 'period' may go on to be identified as positional arguments.

```
    pounds_per_hour = flow_rate(weight_diff, time_diff, 3600,
    2.2)
```

If you think about it, positionally supplying the optional arguments can be very confusing because it is not very clear what the 3600 and 2.2 values are corresponding to. In this case, the best practice is to specify, always, the optional arguments using the keyword names and never passing them as positional arguments.

You need to note that backwards compatibility using such optional keyword arguments is important for functions that accept *args. You can go back to the subtopic discussing reducing visual noise with variable positional arguments. Again, you will find that an even better practice is using keyword only arguments—for this, read more on a subsequent subtopic talking about enforcing clarity with keyword-based arguments.

Things You Need To Remember About Arguments

As you work with arguments, keep in mind the following things:

- ✓ You can specify function arguments by keyword or position

- ✓ Keywords clarify what each argument's purpose is when it could otherwise be confusing when done with positional arguments alone.

- ✓ Keyword arguments that contain default values ease the process of adding fresh behaviors to functions, particularly when the function contains prevailing callers.

- ✓ The optional keyword arguments have to be passed by keyword as opposed to position, always.

Specifying Dynamic Default Arguments using 'none' and Docstrings

At times, you have to use a non-static type as a default value of a keyword argument. For instance, assume you need to print logging messages marked with the logged event time. When it comes to the default case, you will want the messages to have the time when the function was called. You might also want to try the approach below, with the assumption that the default arguments are evaluated again, every time the function is called.

```
def log(message, when=datetime.now()):
    print('%s: %s' % (when, message))

log('Hi there!')
sleep(0.1)
log('Hi again!')

>>>
2014-11-15 21:10:10.371432: Hi there!
2014-11-15 21:10:10.371432: Hi again!
```

The timestamps are similar for the simple reason that the 'datetime.now' is executed only once—that is when the function is defined. The default argument values evaluate once for every module load alone and that typically occurs when a program starts up. Once the module that contains this code is loaded, the default argument 'datetime.now' never evaluates again.

In Python, the convention for accomplishing the wanted result is providing a default 'none' value and documenting the actual docstring behavior. In instances where your code sees a 'none' argument value, you then allot the default value fittingly.

```
def log(message, when=None):
    """Log a message with a timestamp.

    Args:
        message: Message to print.
        when: datetime of when the message occurred.
            Defaults to the present time.
    """
    when = datetime.now() if when is None else when
    print('%s: %s' % (when, message))
```

At this point, the timestamps will not be the same.

```
log('Hi there!')
sleep(0.1)
log('Hi again!')
```

```
>>>
2014-11-15 21:10:10.472303: Hi there!
2014-11-15 21:10:10.573395: Hi again!
```

When you use 'none' for the default argument values, it is particularly important whenever such arguments are variable or mutable. For instance, you need to load a value that has been encoded as JSON data. If there happens to be a fail in decoding the data, you will need an empty dictionary to be returned. You might thus want to try the approach below:

```
def decode(data, default={}):
    try:
        return json.loads(data)
    except ValueError:
        return default
```

The issue here is similar to the example above with 'datetime.now'. The 'default' specified dictionary will need to be shared by all for decoding since the default argument values are, at module load time, evaluated only once. This can bring about a very surprising behavior.

```
foo = decode('bad data')
foo['stuff'] = 5
bar = decode('also bad')
bar['meep'] = 1
print('Foo:', foo)
print('Bar:', bar)
```

```
>>>
Foo: {'stuff': 5, 'meep': 1}
Bar: {'stuff': 5, 'meep': 1}
```

In this case, you would be expecting two distinct dictionaries that both contain one key and value. Nonetheless, modifying one of them would also seem to modify the other. The problem is that 'foo' and 'bar' are equal to the parameter 'default'. Both are identical dictionary object as you can see.

assert foo is bar

To fix this, you will need to set the keyword argument default value to 'none'; after that, you will need to start documenting the behavior in the docstring of the function.

```
def decode(data, default=None):
    """Load JSON data from a string.

    Args:
        data: JSON data to decode.
        default: Value to return if decoding fails.
            Defaults to an empty dictionary.
    """
    if default is None:
        default = {}
    try:
        return json.loads(data)
    except ValueError:
            return default
```

At this point, when you run the same test code as before, you will get the expected result.

```
foo = decode('bad data')
foo['stuff'] = 5
bar = decode('also bad')
bar['meep'] = 1
print('Foo:', foo)
print('Bar:', bar)


>>>
Foo: {'stuff': 5}
    Bar: {meep': 1}
```

Do not forget the following:

- ✓ Default arguments are evaluated only once during the function definition at the module load time. Well, this can bring about odd behaviors for the dynamic values such as [] or {}.

- ✓ For the keyword arguments containing a dynamic value, you can use 'none' as the default value. Now document the definite default behavior in the docstring of the function.

Enforcing Clarity with Keyword-Only Arguments

A powerful feature in the functions of Python is passing arguments by keyword. The flexibility given by the keyword arguments makes it possible to write code that will be clear for use cases.

For instance, you need to divide a single number by another but are at the same time careful about the special cases. At times, you need to ignore the exceptions: 'ZeroDivisionError' and instead return infinity. Again, you will want to ignore the exceptions: 'OverflowError' and instead return zero.

```python
def safe_division(number, divisor, ignore_overflow,
        ignore_zero_division):
  try:
    return number / divisor
  except OverflowError:
    if ignore_overflow:
      return 0
    else:
      raise
  except ZeroDivisionError:
    if ignore_zero_division:
      return float('inf')
    else:
        raise
```

You will note that this function is straightforward and the call will thus ignore the overflow 'float' from division and return zero as a result.

```
result = safe_division(1, 10**500, True, False)
print(result)

>>>
    0.0
```

This call ignores the error arising from dividing by zero and returns infinity.

```
result = safe_division(1, 0, False, True)
print(result)

>>>
    inf
```

The issue here is that it is quite easy to confuse the exact position of both Boolean arguments controlling the behavior ignoring the exception. This could easily bring about bugs that are very difficult to track down. A good way to increase the code's readability is using the keyword arguments. By default, the function can be extremely cautious and continually re-raise exceptions.

```
def safe_division_b(number, divisor,
        ignore_overflow=False,
        ignore_zero_division=False):
    # ...
```

The callers can then use keyword arguments to specify the kind of ignore flags they need to flip for particular operations to override the default behavior.

```
safe_division_b(1, 10**500, ignore_overflow=True)
    safe_division_b(1, 0, ignore_zero_division=True)
```

The keyword arguments are essentially optional behavior, such that there is nothing forcing your functions' callers to use the keyword arguments for clarity. With positional arguments, you can still be able to call it the old way even with the new 'safe_division_b' definition.

```
safe_division_b(1, 10**500, True, False)
```

With such complex function, you will want to require that callers have their intentions clear. In Python, you can demand clarity by making sure you define your functions with keyword-only arguments. Such arguments cannot be supplied by position, only by keyword.

In this case, you redefine the function 'safe_division' such that it accepts keyword-only arguments. The asterisk * in the argument list designates the end of positional arguments and the start of keyword-only arguments.

```
def safe_division_c(number, divisor, *,
            ignore_overflow=False,
            ignore_zero_division=False):
    # ...
```

At this point, it will not be workable to call the function for the keyword argument with positional arguments.

```
safe_division_c(1, 10**500, True, False)
```

```
>>>
TypeError: safe_division_c() takes 2 positional arguments but 4
were given
```

Keyword arguments and their default values work as expected.

```
safe_division_c(1, 0, ignore_zero_division=True) # OK

try:
  safe_division_c(1, 0)
except ZeroDivisionError:
        pass # Expected
```

Python 2's Keyword-Only Arguments

Unfortunately, unlike Python 3, Python 2 does not have an explicit syntax for specifying keyword-only arguments. Nonetheless, you can still attain the same behavior of getting 'TypeErrors' for function calls that are not valid with the operator '**' in the argument lists. This operator is the same as the * operator. The only difference being that it takes whichever number of keyword arguments instead of taking a variable number of positional arguments regardless of the fact that they may not be defined.

```
# Python 2
def print_args(*args, **kwargs):
  print 'Positional:', args
  print 'Keyword: ', kwargs

print_args(1, 2, foo='bar', stuff='meep')

>>>
Positional: (1, 2)
    Keyword:   {'foo': 'bar', 'stuff': 'meep'}
```

If you want to have 'safe_division' take arguments that are keyword-only in Python 2, you need to have the function take **kwargs. After that, you 'pop' the expected keyword arguments—that is, out of the kwargs dictionary with the second argument of the 'pop' method to lay down the default value when the key is not there. Lastly, you will need to ensure there are no more keyword arguments remaining in kwargs so that the callers do not supply invalid arguments.

```python
# Python 2
def safe_division_d(number, divisor, **kwargs):
    ignore_overflow = kwargs.pop('ignore_overflow', False)
    ignore_zero_div = kwargs.pop('ignore_zero_division', False)
    if kwargs:
        raise TypeError('Unexpected **kwargs: %r' % kwargs)
        # ...
```

You can now call the function using or without using the keyword arguments.

```python
safe_division_d(1, 10)
safe_division_d(1, 0, ignore_zero_division=True)
    safe_division_d(1, 10**500, ignore_overflow=True)
```

Just as is the case with Python 3, it will not be workable to passing keyword-only arguments.

```python
safe_division_d(1, 0, False, True)
```

```python
>>>
TypeError: safe_division_d() takes 2 positional arguments but 4 were given
```

Trying to pass unexpected keyword arguments also won't work.

```python
safe_division_d(0, 0, unexpected=True)
```

```python
>>>
    TypeError: Unexpected **kwargs: {'unexpected': True}
```

Do not forget the following:

- ✓ Keyword arguments usually make a function's intention clearer.

- ✓ You could use keyword-only arguments to enable you to force callers to actually supply keyword arguments for any function that is potentially confusing. This particularly applies to those that accept more than a single multiple Boolean flag.

- ✓ Python 3 abets explicit syntax for arguments that are keyword-only in functions.

- ✓ Python 2 can imitate arguments that are keyword-only for functions with **kwargs and raising 'TypeError' exceptions manually.

Namespaces in Python

In real life, name conflicts occur all the time. For instance, most schools you have attended have had no less than two students sharing the first name. For instance, when a teacher asked for student Y, most of the other students would enthusiastically inquire about the one he or she is talking about (since perhaps there are two students with the name Y). After that, in this case, the teacher would give a last name and the right Y would respond.

You would agree that if everyone had a special name, all the confusion here and process of determining the right person talked about by seeking out additional information alongside a first name would be easy to avoid. In a class that has 20 or 30 students, this may not be a problem. However, in a school, city, town—or even a country—it may not be possible to create a unique, relevant, and simple-to-remember name for all the kids in those areas. Moreover, another problem would be making sure we give each child a unique name; that is determining whether someone else has a name with the same pronunciation as a given name (for instance Macie, Maci, or Macey).

Programming may also face a very similar conflict.

When a programmer is writing a 30-line program without any external dependencies, it is very easy for him or her to provide unique and relevant names to all the variables. However, similarly, when there are a few thousand lines in the program and perhaps some external modules loaded as well, there arises a problem—*Modules are files that contain the definitions and statements of Python.* This brings to us to our topic of Namespaces.

In this section, you will understand why they are important and scope resolution in Python:

Meaning of Namespaces

A namespace is a system of making sure all program names are special unique and you, the programmer, can use them without causing any conflict. By now, you should know very well that all Python stuff such as functions, lists, and strings are objects. Well, you may want to know Python usually makes use of namespaces as dictionaries. We have a name-to-object mapping with objects as values and names as keys. Many different namespaces can actually use one name and then proceed to map it to a distinct object.

Look at the following namespace examples.

Local namespaces: These namespaces comprise local names within a function. The creation of such namespaces happens when functions are called, and only last up until the functions return.

Global namespaces: These namespaces comprise names from different imported modules used in a project. Their creation happens when the modules are incorporated into the project and stick around only before the scripts end.

Built-in namespaces: These namespaces consist of built-in exception names and built-in functions.

Even though we will discuss modules in a later chapter, you need to note that there are useful arithmetic functions in different modules. For instance, the cmath and math modules contain many functions that are shared in the two, such as acos(), exp(), cos(), log10() and so on. If you use both modules in one program, you will need to prefix them with the module's name if you want to be able to use the functions unambiguously—for instance, cmath.log10() and math.log10().

Scope

Namespaces are important because for one, they identify the whole list of names within a program. Nonetheless, this does not necessarily imply that variable names can be used anywhere. A name also contains a scope defining the sections of the program that the name would be used without the use of any prefix.

Similar to namespaces, we also have many scopes in a program. Look at the following list of a number of scopes that can be in the course of a program execution.

- ✓ Local scope: The local scope is the innermost scope containing a list of local names that are available in the existing function.

- ✓ The scope of the whole enclosing functions. A name search begins from the enclosing scope that is nearest, moving outwards.

- ✓ A module level scope containing the entire list of global names from the existing module and

- ✓ The outermost scope containing the entire list of built-in names—this scope is usually searched last to get the referenced name.

Scope Resolution

As we have already seen, a search for a particular name begins from the innermost function before moving higher until the name is mapped to the object (by the program). In cases where the program does not find such name within the namespaces, the program then raises what's referred to as a NameError exception. As we start, try to type 'dir ()' in a python IDE such as IDLE.

```
dir()
# ['__builtins__','__doc__','__loader__','__name__',
'__package__','__spec__']
```

All the names are listed by dir() are offered in all Python programs. Just to be brief, I will, in the other examples, begin by referring to these names as '__builtins__'...'__specs__'.

Let us see the result of the dir() function once we define a variable and a function.

```
a_num = 10
dir()
# ['__builtins__' ....'__spec__', 'a_num']

def some_func():
    b_num = 11
    print(dir())

some_func()
# ['b_num']

dir()
# ['__builtins__' ...'__spec__', 'a_num', 'some_func'
```

The function 'dir()' outputs the name list within the existing scope. This is exactly why there is just a single name named b_num within the 'some_func()' scope. When you call 'dir()' after you define 'some_func()', you get it added to the name list present in the global namespace.

We will now look at the name list within some nested functions. Note that the code present in this block goes on from the previous block.

```
def outer_func():
    c_num = 12
    def inner_func():
        d_num = 13
        print(dir(), ' - names in inner_func')
    e_num = 14
    inner_func()
    print(dir(), ' - names in outer_func')

outer_func()
# ['d_num'] - names in inner_func
# ['c_num', 'e_num', 'inner_func'] - names in outer_func
```

The code above is defining two variables and one function within the 'outer_func()' scope. The 'dir()' only prints the 'd_num' name within the 'inner_func()'. Since there is no other variable defined in there apart from 'd_num', it is fair.

When we reassign a global name within a local namespace, we create a new local variable containing the same name; this is so unless plainly specified with global. The code below describes this more evidently.

```
a_num = 10
b_num = 11

def outer_func():
    global a_num
    a_num = 15
    b_num = 16
    def inner_func():
        global a_num
        a_num = 20
        b_num = 21
        print('a_num inside inner_func :', a_num)
        print('b_num inside inner_func :', b_num)
```

```
  inner_func()
  print('a_num inside outer_func :', a_num)
  print('b_num inside outer_func :', b_num)

outer_func()
print('a_num outside all functions :', a_num)
print('b_num outside all functions :', b_num)

# a_num inside inner_func : 20
# b_num inside inner_func : 21

# a_num inside outer_func : 20
# b_num inside outer_func : 16

# a_num outside all functions : 20
# b_num outside all functions : 11
```

'a_num' has been declared within the 'outer_func()' and also 'inner_func()' to be a global variable. A different value is just being set for a similar global variable. It is for this reason that the 'a_num' value is 20 at all locations. Each function, on the other hand, builds its own variable 'b_num' with a local scope; the function 'print()' then prints this locally scoped variable's value.

Python Modules

We use modules to categorize the code in Python into smaller parts. Essentially, in Python, a module is a Python file in which variables, functions, and classes are defined. When you group the same code into one file, you essentially make it easy to access. This is what modules mean. For instance, we have categorized or indexed the content in this book into various chapters so that it does not become boring or hectic. This means that by dividing the book into chapters, the content becomes easier to understand and navigate.

In the same vein, modules are the files that contain the same code.

Importing a Module

There are ways of importing modules. They include the following:

1: *Using* Import Statement

You can use the 'import' statement for the importation. Take the example of the syntax below:

```
1. import <file_name1, file_name2,...file_name(n)="">
2. </file_name1,>
```

The following is an example:

```
1. def add(a,b):
2.    c=a+b
3.    print c
4.    return
```

You can save the file under the name 'addition.py'. You will use the 'import' statement to import this file.

1. import addition
2. addition.add(10,20)
3. addition.add(30,40)

Now build another file in Python where you want to import the former file. For that, you will use the import statement as you have seen in the example above. You can use 'file_name.method()' for the corresponding method. In this case, we have addition.add (). Here, Addition is the file in Python, and add () is the method defined in the addition.py file.

The output is as follows:

1. >>>
2. 30
3. 70
4. >>>

You need to note that you can access any function within a module by the function name and module name disjointed by a dot. This is termed as a period. A whole notation is referred to as dot notation.

An example of Python Importing Multiple Modules

Msg.py:

1. def msg_method():
2.   print "Today the weather is rainy"
3.   return

display.py:

```
1. def display_method():
2.    print "The weather is Sunny"
```

return

multiimport.py:

```
1. import msg,display
2. msg.msg_method()
3. display.display_method()
```

The output is as follows:

```
1. >>>
2. Today the weather is rainy
3. The weather is Sunny
```

>>>

2: Use of from..import statement

We use the from..import statement to import certain attributes from modules. In case you do not need the entire module imported, you can simply use the from? Import statement. The syntax is as follows:

Syntax:

```
1. from <module_name> import <attribute1,attribute2,attribu
   te3,...attributen>
2. </attribute1,attribute2,attribute3,...attributen></module_n
   ame>
```

An example of Python from..import

```
1. def circle(r):
2.    print 3.14*r*r
3.    return
4.
5. def square(l):
6.    print l*l
7.    return
8.
9. def rectangle(l,b):
10.        print l*b
11.        return
12.
13.     def triangle(b,h):
14.        print 0.5*b*h
15.        return
```

area1.py

```
1. from area import square,rectangle
2. square(10)
3. rectangle(2,5)
```

The output is as follows:

```
1. >>>
2. 100
3. 10
4. >>>
```

3: Importing Whole Modules

You can import the entire module with 'from? Import*'. The syntax is as follows:

```
1. from <module_name> import *
2. </module_name>
```

With the statement above, the entire list of attributes defined in the module will be imported and thus, you can be able to access every attribute.

area.py

This is same as the example above:

area1.py

```
1. from area import *
2. square(10)
3. rectangle(2,5)
4. circle(5)
5. triangle(10,20)
```

The output is as follows:

```
1. >>>
2. 100
3. 10
4. 78.5
5. 100.0
6. >>>
```

Built In Python Modules

In Python, we have numerous built in modules; some of them include the following: random, math, collections, threading, mailbox, os, time, string, tkinter, and so on.

Each module contains some built in functions you can use to perform different functions. Here is a look at two modules:

1: Math

With the math module, you can use the various built in arithmetic functions.

The functions and their descriptions include the following:

Function	Description
ceil(n)	It returns the next integer number of the given number
sqrt(n)	It returns the Square root of the given number.
exp(n)	It returns the natural logarithm e raised to the given number
floor(n)	It returns the previous integer number of the given number.
log(n,baseto)	It returns the natural logarithm of the number.
pow(baseto, exp)	It returns baseto raised to the exp power.
sin(n)	It returns sine of the given radian.
cos(n)	It returns cosine of the given radian.
tan(n)	It returns tangent of the given radian.

An example of a math module

```
1. import math
2. a=4.6
3. print math.ceil(a)
4. print math.floor(a)
5. b=9
6. print math.sqrt(b)
7. print math.exp(3.0)
```

8. print math.log(2.0)
9. print math.pow(2.0,3.0)
10.   print math.sin(0)
11.   print math.cos(0)
12.   print math.tan(45)

The output is as follows:

1. >>>
2. 5.0
3. 4.0
4. 3.0
5. 20.0855369232
6. 0.69314718056
7. 8.0
8. 0.0
9. 1.0
10.   1.61977519054
11.   >>>

Again, the math module gives two constants for arithmetic operations as follows:

Constants	Descriptions
Pi	Returns constant ? = 3.14159…
ceil(n)	Returns constant e= 2.71828…

Look at the example below:

1. import math
2.
3. print math.pi
4. print math.e

The output is as follows:

1. >>>
2. 3.14159265359
3. 2.71828182846
4. >>>

2: Random

We use the random module to generate random numbers. It gives these two built-in functions:

Function	Description
random()	It returns a random number between 0.0 and 1.0 where 1.0 is exclusive.
randint(x,y)	It returns a random number between x and y where both the numbers are inclusive.

An example of the Python Module

1. import random
2.
3. print random.random()
4. print random.randint(2,8)

The output is as follows:

1. >>>
2. 0.797473843839
3. 7
4. >>>

Having looked at most of the things you need to learn at this intermediate level, we shall look at example Python projects that when practiced, should help you implement the knowledge you have learnt thus far in this guide:

Simple Python projects for Intermediates

Having covered all the topics relevant at an intermediate level, I believe you are prepared to take on a few projects of your own. First, let us look at a few project examples to give you a head start!

1: Scrabble Challenge

In this project, you will create a scrabble cheater.

The goals of this project include the following:

- ✓ Practicing to break a problem down and solve it from scratch in Python

- ✓ Practicing the command line argument parsing

- ✓ Practicing to read from Python files

- ✓ Practicing to work with for loops and dictionaries

Essentially, you write a script in Python that assumes a Scrabble rack to be a command-line argument before printing all the valid Scrabble words that are buildable from the rack along with their respective scores on Scrabble–(these ought to be sorted by score). Take the example invocation below, and output.

```
[[Media:]]
$ python scrabble.py ZAEFIEE
17 feeze
17 feaze
16 faze
15 fiz
15 fez
12 zee
12 zea
11 za
6 fie
6 fee
6 fae
5 if
5 fe
5 fa
5 ef
2 ee
2 ea
2 ai
2 ae
```

The site in this link has all the words in the SOWPODS word list (official) a single word per line.

Look at the dictionary below—it contains all the letters and their values in scrabble:

```
scores = {"a": 1, "c": 3, "b": 3, "e": 1, "d": 2, "g": 2,
    "f": 4, "i": 1, "h": 4, "k": 5, "j": 8, "m": 3,
    "l": 1, "o": 1, "n": 1, "q": 10, "p": 3, "s": 1,
    "r": 1, "u": 1, "t": 1, "w": 4, "v": 4, "y": 4,
    "x": 8, "z": 10}
```

Let us try to break the problem down.

Create a Word List

Write your code to open and read the word file 'sowpods'. Build a list where every element is essentially a word in the word file 'sowpods'. You need to note that every line in the file is ending in a new line, which you will have to eliminate from the word.

Get the rack

Write your code to acquire the scrabble rack (these are the letters present to create words) from the command line argument passed to your script. For instance, say your script was known as 'scrabble_cheater.py', if you tend to run *'python scrabble_cheater.py RSTLNEI*, the rack would then be RSTLNEI.

Try handling the case when a user is forgetting to supply a rack—in which case, print the error message that states that they have to supply certain letters; now exit the program with the function 'exit ()'. Ensure you maintain consistency when it comes to capitalization.

Now get valid words

Now write the code, which will help you to get every word in the Scrabble word list, which is made of letters that are a subdivision of the different rack letters. You can do this in many ways. However, you can use one way that is simple to reason about but is fast enough for your purpose here: go over every word in the word list and see whether every letter is in the rack. If you find it is, save the word in a list: 'valid_words'. Ensure to handle the repeat letters; a letter from the rack cannot be used once more when it has already been used.

The scoring

Now write the code that will help you determine the scrabble scores for every valid word with the above scores dictionary.

Check your work

In this step, ask yourself what would happen if you ran your script on the outputs below:

```
$ python scrabble.py
Usage: scrabble.py [RACK]
$ python scrabble.py AAAaaaa
2 aa
$ python scrabble.py ZZAAEEI
22,zeze
21,ziz
12,zee
12,zea
11,za
3,aia
2,ee
2,ea
2,ai
2,aa
2,ae
```

Congratulations! You have just implemented an important and useful script in Python from the beginning; and as you know, it is ideal for cheating at words or scrabble with friends. Do not stop practicing!

2: 'Where Is the Space Station' Project

This project allows you to use a web service to get the present location of the ISS (international space station), and then plot its exact location on a map.

Step 1: Know who is in space

To get started, you are going to use a web service that offers live information about space. We will first try finding out who is in space right now.

You need to note that a web service has a URL or address similar to a typical webpage. However, it returns data instead of returning webpage HTML. In a web browser, open the following link:

http://api.open-notify.org/astros.json

Wait to see something like this:

```
{
  "message": "success",
  "number": 3,
  "people": [
    {
      "craft": "ISS",
      "name": "Yuri Malenchenko"
    },
    {
      "craft": "ISS",
      "name": "Timothy Kopra"
    },
    {
      "craft": "ISS",
      "name": "Timothy Peake"
    }
  ]
}
```

Since the data is live, you will definitely see a very different result. We call this format JSON.

We will now call the web service from Python to be able to use the results. Open the trinket below:

jumpto.cc/iss-go.

The modules: 'json' and 'urllib.request' are imported and are ready for your use. Now add the code below to 'main.py' to be able to place the web address you used earlier into a variable:

```
url = 'http://api.open-notify.org/astros.json'
```

We will now call the web service as follows:

```
url = 'http://api.open-notify.org/astros.json'
response = urllib.request.urlopen(url)
```

After that, we will have to have the JSON response loaded into a Python data structure as follows:

```
url = 'http://api.open-notify.org/astros.json'
response = urllib.request.urlopen(url)
result = json.loads(response.read())
print(result)
```

In this case, you should be able to see something like:

{'message': 'success', 'number': 3, 'people': [{'craft': 'ISS', 'name': 'Yuri Malenchenko'}, {'craft': 'ISS', 'name': 'Timothy Kopra'}, {'craft': 'ISS', 'name': 'Timothy Peake'}]}

This is simply a Python dictionary containing three keys that include people, number, and message. The value 'success' of the message shows that the request was successful.

Nonetheless, you need to note that depending on who is currently in space, you will see different results.

We will now try printing the information in a more readable manner: First, let us try looking up the total number of people currently in space and print it as follows:

```
url = 'http://api.open-notify.org/astros.json'
response = urllib.request.urlopen(url)
result = json.loads(response.read())

print('People in Space: ', result['number'])
```

The value related to the 'number' key in the result dictionary will be printed by result['number']. In the case here, it is 3.

The value related to the key 'people' is a dictionaries' list. We will try putting that value into a variable so that you can be able to use it as follows:

```
print('People in Space: ', result['number'])

people = result['people']
print(people)
```

You will see something that looks like this:

[{'craft': 'ISS', 'name': 'Yuri Malenchenko'}, {'craft': 'ISS', 'name': 'Timothy Kopra'}, {'craft': 'ISS', 'name': 'Timothy Peake'}]

You will now have to print out lines for all astronauts—one for each. To achieve this, you can easily use a for loop. 'p' will be set to a dictionary each time through the loop for a distinct astronaut.

```
print('People in Space: ', result['number'])

people = result['people']

for p in people:
  print(p)
```

You can now try looking up the values for 'craft' and 'name'.

```
print('People in Space: ', result['number'])

people = result['people']

for p in people:
  print(p['name'])
```

In this case, you will see something that looks like this:

People in Space: 3
Yuri Malenchenko
Timothy Kopra
Timothy Peake

You need to note that you are using live data; thus, your results are dependent on the number of people currently in space.

Show the craft: challenge

The web service also gives the craft they are in–like the ISS apart from the name of the astronaut. You can add to the script so that the craft the astronaut is in also prints out.

Take the example below:

People in Space: 3
Yuri Malenchenko in ISS
Timothy Kopra in ISS
Timothy Peake in ISS

Step 2: Find the ISS Location

The ISS is always going around or orbiting earth. It does so (orbits) after about one and a half hours. It also travels an average of 7.66 kilometers per second, which means it is very fast.

You will use a different web service to know where the ISS is right now. In your browser, open the URL below for the web service in a new tab:

http://api.open-notify.org/iss-now.json

You will see something that looks like so:

```
{
"iss_position": {
  "latitude": 8.54938193505081,
  "longitude": 73.16560793639105
},
"message": "success",
"timestamp": 1461931913
}
```

The result has the coordinates of the spot on earth that the ISS is over now. The longitude is the east to west position that runs from (negative) -180 to 180. Zero is the prime meridian running through London (Greenwich) in the UK.

The latitude is the North to South position running from 90 to (negative) -90. In this case, Zero is the equator. You will now have to use Python to actually call the same web service. Add the code below to the finish of your script so that you get the location of the ISS now.

```
url = 'http://api.open-notify.org/iss-now.json'
response = urllib.request.urlopen(url)
result = json.loads(response.read())

print(result)
```

```
{'message': 'success',
'iss_position': {'latitude':
17.0762447364, 'longitude':
66.6454000717}, 'timestamp':
1461931742}
```

You will now build variables to store the longitude and latitude before printing them.

```
url = 'http://api.open-notify.org/iss-now.json'
response = urllib.request.urlopen(url)
result = json.loads(response.read())

location = result['iss_position']
lat = location['latitude']
lon = location['longitude']
print('Latitude: ', lat)
print('Longitude: ', lon)
```

```
Latitude:   26.4169023793
Longitude:  58.378453289
```

As you would guess, it would be better to display its position on the map. To do that, we will have to import the turtle graphics library.

```
import json
import urllib.request
import turtle
```

We will now load a world map as the image background; we have one already included in your trinket. Let us load a world map as the background image.

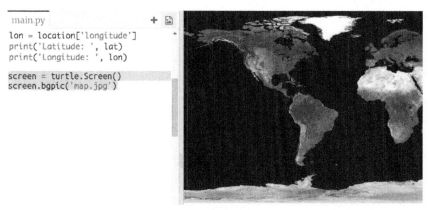

```
main.py                          + 🖼
lon = location['longitude']
print('Latitude: ', lat)
print('Longitude: ', lon)

screen = turtle.Screen()
screen.bgpic('map.jpg')
```

Thanks to NASA, you have this great map—NASA has also provided permission for reuse. The map centers at zero—and zero happens to be just what you require.

Note that you will have to set your screen's size to match the image size. It is 720 by 360.

Include 'screen.setup(720, 360)'

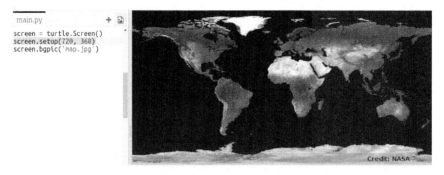

You will want to have the ability to send the turtle to a certain longitude and latitude. You can set the screen to agree with the coordinates you are using to make this simple:

```
screen = turtle.Screen()
screen.setup(720, 360)
screen.setworldcoordinates(-180, -90, 180, 90)
screen.bgpic('map.jpg')
```

The coordinates will now agree with the longitude and latitude coordinates that you get back from the service.

We will now make a turtle for the ISS.

```
screen = turtle.Screen()
screen.setup(720, 360)
screen.setworldcoordinates(-180, -90, 180, 90)
screen.bgpic('map.jpg')

screen.register_shape('iss.png')
iss = turtle.Turtle()
iss.shape('iss.png')
iss.setheading(90)
```

You can try both iss2.png and iss.png in your project to see the one you prefer. The ISS begins in the center of the map. Let us now move it to the right location on the map as follows:

```
screen.register_shape('iss.png')
iss = turtle.Turtle()
iss.shape('iss.png')
iss.setheading(90)

iss.penup()
iss.goto(lon, lat)
```

You need to note that the latitude is usually given first, but when plotting the coordinates x, y, we will have to give the longitude first.

Run the program to test it. The ISS needs to move above earth to its present location.

Take a few seconds before running the program once more to see where the ISS has moved to.

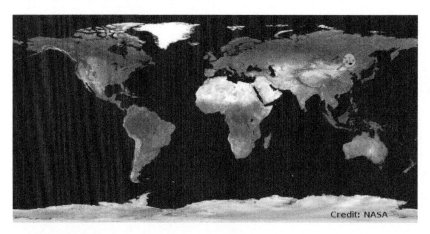
Credit: NASA

```
Latitude:   51.1757114507
Longitude:  119.515729267
```

Step 3: The time the ISS will be overhead

We also have a web service you can call to get the time the ISS will be over a certain location next.

Now try finding out when the ISS will be over the Space Center in Houston, US. This area is at a longitude 95.097 and latitude 29.5502.

On the following coordinates, plot a dot on the map.

```
iss.penup()
iss.goto(lon, lat)

# Space Center, Houston
lat = 29.5502
lon = -95.097

location = turtle.Turtle()
location.penup()
location.color('yellow')
location.goto(lon,lat)
location.dot(5)
location.hideturtle()
```

Let us now get the time and date the ISS is next overhead.

Just like earlier, you can enter the URL into the web browser's address bar to call the web service:

http://api.open-notify.org/iss-pass.json

You will see an error in this case as follows:

```
{
    "message": "failure",
    "reason": "Latitude must be specified"
}
```

The web service is taking longitude and latitude as inputs so we need to include them in the URL we are using.

The inputs are included after a ? and then separated with the & symbol.

Just add the inputs 'lat' and 'lon' to the URL as described:

243

http://api.open-notify.org/iss-pass.json?lat=29.55&lon=95.1

```json
{
  "message": "success",
  "request": {
    "altitude": 100,
    "datetime": 1465541028,
    "latitude": 29.55,
    "longitude": 95.1,
    "passes": 5
  },
  "response": [
    {
      "duration": 630,
      "risetime": 1465545197
    },
    {
      "duration": 545,
      "risetime": 1465551037
    },
    {
      "duration": 382,
      "risetime": 1465568806
    },
    {
      "duration": 625,
      "risetime": 1465574518
    }
  ]
}
```

The response comprises a number pass over times and you will just look at the first one. Again, the time is in a standard time format. You will be able to convert it to a readable time in Python.

Now, try to call the web service from Python. Just add the code below to the close of your script.

```
url = 'http://api.open-notify.org/iss-pass.json'
url = url + '?lat=' + str(lat) + '&lon=' + str(lon)
response = urllib.request.urlopen(url)
result = json.loads(response.read())
print(result)
```

{'message': 'success', 'request':
{'latitude': 29.5502, 'longitude':
-95.097, 'altitude': 100, 'datetime':
1465540436, 'passes': 5}, 'response':
[{'duration': 435, 'risetime':
1465541544}, {'duration': 622,
'risetime': 1465589616}, {'duration':
564, 'risetime': 1465595438},
{'duration': 156, 'risetime':
1465601504}, {'duration': 345,
'risetime': 1465613231}]}

From the result, we will now get the initial pass over time from the result.

Just add the code below:

```
url = 'http://api.open-notify.org/iss-pass.json'
url = url + '?lat=' + str(lat) + '&lon=' + str(lon)
response = urllib.request.urlopen(url)
result = json.loads(response.read())

over = result['response'][1]['risetime']
print(over)
```

1465595438

Pass over time in standard format

The time is as a timestamp; you will thus require the Python time module to be able to print it in a readable form then convert it to the local time. We will have the turtle to write the time of Passover by the dot.

At the top of the script, add a line: 'import time'.

```
import json
import urllib.request
import turtle
import time
```

The function 'time.ctime()' will now convert the time into a readable form that you will equally be able to write with the turtle:

```
over = result['response'][1]['risetime']
#print over

style = ('Arial', 6, 'bold')
location.write(time.ctime(over), font=style)
```

Fri Jun 10 22:50:38

245

Note that you can comment out or remove the line 'print'.

Try to find more Passover times: your challenge

There are websites available for you to use such as <u>this one</u> to look up longitudes and latitudes of places you have particular interests in.

Can you now look up and plot the pass over times for other locations?

- ✓ For one, you will have to change the longitude and latitude inputs to the web service.

- ✓ You will also have to plot the location and outcome on the map.

3: Creating a simple Keylogger

Do you know what a keylogger is? In case you do not, here is a little bit of introduction.

Also known as keystroke logging, a keylogger is some sort of surveillance software that has the ability to record every keystroke made on a computer system it is installed in. The recording is then saved in a typically encrypted log file.

A keylogger can record email, instant messages, and get any information typed anytime using the computer's keyboard—this includes passwords, usernames, and other pii (personally identifiable information). The keylogger creates the log file and then sends it to a specific receiver. A number of keylogger programs also record any email addresses used as well as the URLs of the websites visited.

What is the use of keyloggers?

As a surveillance tool, employers normally use keyloggers to make sure employees are using work computers for purposes of business only. We also have an increasing market of parents looking to use keyloggers to remain informed about the online activities of their children.

It is rather unfortunate that some programmers embed keyloggers in spyware; this means it could allow the transmission of your personal information to an anonymous third party.

In any case, you see it (keyloggers) on the internet, and maybe even have downloaded or installed it at some point in your life—or seen someone doing it at least—whether to monitor or spy on someone or something like that. Windows 10 actually contains an in-built keylogger.

As you might have already guessed though, the process of installing this software might come with various dangerous viruses. This is perhaps one of the reasons why creating your own is the best option.

Let us briefly go over the steps of creating a keylogger.

Step 1: Install python

Having an operational python program is obvious; and unless you already have downloaded a file with a pre-compiled keylogger, you need to install Python alongside a couple of modules. Download and install these modules:

- ✓ Latest Python version
- ✓ Pywin32
- ✓ PyHook

Step 2: Create the code

```
import pyHook, pythoncom, sys, logging
file_log = 'keyloggeroutput.txt'
def OnKeyboardEvent(event):
    logging.basicConfig(filename=file_log, level=logging.DEBUG, format='%(m
    chr(event.Ascii)
    logging.log(10,chr(event.Ascii))
    return True
hooks_manager = pyHook.HookManager()
hooks_manager.KeyDown = OnKeyboardEvent
hooks_manager.HookKeyboard()
pythoncom.PumpMessages()
```

When you have had all the Python stuff fully installed, open up IDLE, build a new script, and then enter in the code below:

import pyHook, pythoncom, sys, logging

feel free to set the file_log to a different file name/location

file_log = 'keyloggeroutput.txt'

def OnKeyboardEvent(event):
  logging.basicConfig(filename=file_log, level=logging.DEBUG, format='%(message)s')
    chr(event.Ascii)
    logging.log(10,chr(event.Ascii))
    return True
hooks_manager = pyHook.HookManager()
hooks_manager.KeyDown = OnKeyboardEvent
hooks_manager.HookKeyboard()
pythoncom.PumpMessages()

Now save this as something.pyw

248

Step 3: Test

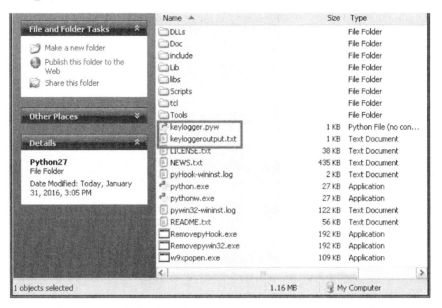

Now open the file you just created and test it out; now start typing. When you want to stop logging, you can simply open up the task manager and kill all the processes in 'Python'. After that go to the same directory where something.pyw is and look for keyloggeroutput.txt. Now open it to see all that you typed.

You need to note that you could see a bit of weird looking character if you try opening it using notepad; those characters mean you press backspace.

I would say that this is the end of this discussion because that is pretty much what you need to know. However, I think you still need to see one keylogger (as an example) to understand this even better. So, let us continue.

Step 4: observe the keylogger example below

File	Size	Type	Date
_hashlib.pyd	889 KB	PYD File	2015-05-23 9:41 AM
_win32sysloader.pyd	8 KB	PYD File	2014-05-03 12:56 PM
bz2.pyd	67 KB	PYD File	2015-05-23 9:40 AM
library.zip	1,617 KB	WinRAR ZIP archive	2015-11-23 4:46 PM
pyHook._cpyHook.pyd	27 KB	PYD File	2010-08-27 5:55 AM
python27.dll	2,402 KB	Application Extension	2015-05-23 9:40 AM
pythoncom27.dll	388 KB	Application Extension	2014-05-03 12:59 PM
pywintypes27.dll	108 KB	Application Extension	2014-05-03 12:55 PM
Run.vbs	1 KB	VBScript Script File	2016-01-30 6:13 PM
select.pyd	10 KB	PYD File	2015-05-23 9:41 AM
unicodedata.pyd	670 KB	PYD File	2015-05-23 9:40 AM
winupdate.exe	19 KB	Application	2015-11-23 4:46 PM

First, extract the keylogger.rar and open up the folder containing the files. You should be able to see some random files—this is so because when you compile a Python program to a standalone.exe, you require all the files here in the same directory as the program.

The only significant files include 'winupdate.exe' and 'Run.vbs'. The former is the actual keylogger program labeled as 'winupdate' so that nothing appears suspicious if the user opens up the task manager.

In the instance, you compile a Python program to an .exe, for some reason, you do not have the choice to make it run invisibly. To fix this, you can create a little vbscript file known as Run.vbs that invisibly launches the winupdate.exe.

Step 5: test

Open Run.vbs by double clicking on it and the program will automatically start. If you want to stop logging, just open the task manager up then kill the winupdate.exe. After that, open the keyloggeroutput.txt up to see that all the characters you entered are logged.

As I mentioned earlier, you need to note that you may see a couple of weird looking characters when you open it with notepad. These characters indicate that you have to press the backspace key.

These few simple projects are ones you should be able to handle, and improve on your own using the stuff you learnt in this book. I encourage you to look for more projects such as the password generator programs and codecrafting 3D games on the internet and learn how the Python themes and topics we have covered so far since the beginner's edition are relevant.

Conclusion

We have come to the end of the book. Thank you for reading and congratulations for reading until the end.

I hope you had a great time learning new stuff from the book because I can say I have enjoyed myself so much I just wished I could continue. Sadly, we have to stop here or the next 'advanced' edition would be pointless☺.

In this book, we have covered seven key areas including:

✓ Shallow copy/deep copy

✓ Objects and classes in Python

✓ Recursion in Python

✓ Debugging and testing

✓ Fibonacci sequence and Memoization in Python

✓ Arguments in Python

✓ Namespaces and Python Modules, and summed up with:

✓ Simple Python projects for Intermediates

Each of the topics should take no more than a day to cover so that you can learn everything in this guide within seven (or less) days.

Make sure you get the next book of this series where we shall talk about many other exciting Python topics to ensure you have all the knowledge you ultimately require to be the best in the language.

If you found the book valuable, can you recommend it to others? One way to do that is to post a review on Amazon.

Click here to leave a review for this book on Amazon!

Thank you and good luck!

Python Programming for Advanced

Learn The Basics Of Python In 7 Days!

Maurice J. Thompson

information is without contract or any type of guarantee assurance.

The trademarks that are used are without any consent, and the publication of the trademark is without permission or backing by the trademark owner. All trademarks and brands within this book are for clarifying purposes only and are the owned by the owners themselves, not affiliated with this document.

Table of Contents

Introduction

I want to thank you and congratulate you for buying the book, *"Python Programming for Advanced: Learn The Basics of Python in 1 week!"*.

This book has actionable information that will help you to understand python at an advanced level.

Welcome to the final issue of our Python programming book series. This book is the advanced edition that you have been building up to as you went through the exercises in the last two books. This third issue of the book is even more comprehensive than the previous editions but equally educative and illuminating.

As you walk into the first chapter, just smile as you read and learn, knowing that you are just a single step away from excellence.

In this book, we will continue from where we left off in the last 'intermediates' book. In this guide, will learn/cover the following:

✓ File management

✓ Python Iterator

✓ Python Generator

✓ Regular Expressions

✓ Python Closure

✓ Python Property

✓ Python Assert, and

261

✓ Simple recap projects

As always, I hope you have fun because programming ought to be fun! Let's begin.

Thanks again for downloading this book. I hope you enjoy it!

File Management in Python

In Python, file management is integral in many applications and is indeed one of the most basic functions. Luckily and quite surprisingly, the Python language makes file management simple, especially when you compare it to other languages.

When you, for instance, play a game, its "saves" are stored with the help of files. An order you place is saved in a file. A project report you want to type will also be stored in a file. File management plays a very important role in many applications written in almost all languages; Python is not an exception to this.

In this chapter, we will have a detailed analysis of the task of manipulating files with a number of modules. You will read, append, write to, and do other things to files.

Let us begin.

File Manipulation: Reading and Writing Files in Python

In file manipulation, the basic tasks include writing data to files and reading data from files. This is one of the simplest tasks to learn and perform. Try opening a file for writing:

```
fileHandle = open ( 'test.txt', 'w' )
```

In the example above, 'w' shows you are going to write the file; everything else is quite simple to understand. After that, the next step is writing data to the file - as follows:

```
fileHandle.write ( 'This is a test.nReally, it is.' )
```

From this, we will have s string with the phrases 'this is a test.' to the first line of the file and to the second line, we will have 'Really, it is.' Lastly, you have to clean up after yourself and select the file below:

fileHandle.close()

Well, you can see that this is very simple especially with the object orientation programming that is part of Python. You need to note that when you are using the 'w' mode to write to the file once more, its entire contents are erased. You can use the 'a' mode to get past this; this mode will append data to a file and add data to the bottom:

fileHandle = open ('test.txt', 'a')

fileHandle.write ('nnnBottom line.')

fileHandle.close()

Let us now read the file and display its contents as follows:

fileHandle = open ('test.txt')

print fileHandle.read()

fileHandle.close()

This reads the whole file and prints the data inside it. You can read one line in the file as well:

fileHandle = open ('test.txt')

print fileHandle.readline() # "This is a test."

fileHandle.close()

It is also possible to store the lines of a file into a list:

fileHandle = open ('test.txt')

```
fileList = fileHandle.readlines()
for fileLine in fileList:
  print '>>', fileLine
fileHandle.close()
```

When reading a file, the commands will remember Python's place in it. Look at the example below:

```
fileHandle = open ( 'test.txt' )
garbage = fileHandle.readline()
fileHandle.readline() # "Really, it is."
fileHandle.close()
```

Only the second line displays. You can get past this by informing Python to go back to reading from another position:

```
fileHandle = open ( 'test.txt' )
garbage = fileHandle.readline()
fileHandle.seek ( 0 )
print fileHandle.readline() # "This is a test."
fileHandle.close()
```

In the example above, you are telling Python to keep reading from the file's first byte. Therefore, the first line prints out. You can also ask the place of Python inside the file as follows:

```
fileHandle = open ( 'test.txt' )

print fileHandle.readline() # "This is a test."

print fileHandle.tell() # "17"

print fileHandle.readline() # "Really, it is."
```

It is also possible to read the file a few bytes at a time:

```
fileHandle = open ( 'test.txt' )

print fileHandle.read ( 1 ) # "T"

fileHandle.seek ( 4 )

print FileHandle.read ( 1 ) # "T"
```

When you are working with Macintosh and Windows, you may sometimes need to read and write files in binary mode—files such as executional files or images. To achieve this, you can just append 'b' to the file mode as follows:

```
fileHandle = open ( 'testBinary.txt', 'wb' )

fileHandle.write ( 'There is no spoon.' )

fileHandle.close()
```

```
fileHandle = open ( 'testBinary.txt', 'rb' )

print fileHandle.read()

fileHandle.close()
```

{mospagebreak title=Getting Information on Existing Files}

When you are using a number of modules in Python, you can get information on existing files. You can use the 'os' module together with the 'stat' module to obtain basic information:

```
import os

import stat

import time

fileStats = os.stat ( 'test.txt' )

fileInfo = {

  'Size' : fileStats [ stat.ST_SIZE ],

  'LastModified' : time.ctime ( fileStats [ stat.ST_MTIME ] ),

  'LastAccessed' : time.ctime ( fileStats [ stat.ST_ATIME ] ),

  'CreationTime' : time.ctime ( fileStats [ stat.ST_CTIME ] ),

  'Mode' : fileStats [ stat.ST_MODE ]

}

for infoField, infoValue in fileInfo:

  print infoField, ':' + infoValue

if stat.S_ISDIR ( fileStats [ stat.ST_MODE ] ):

  print 'Directory. '

else:

  print 'Non-directory.'
```

The example above builds a dictionary that has some basic information concerning the file. It then displays the data and informs you whether it is a directory on not. You can also check to find out whether the file is one of the other types:

```
import os

import stat

fileStats = os.stat ( 'test.txt' )

fileMode = fileStats [ stat.ST_MODE ]

if stat.S_ISREG ( fileStats [ stat.ST_MODE ] ):

  print 'Regular file.'

elif stat.S_ISDIR ( fileSTats [ stat.ST_MODe ] ):
```

267

```
  print 'Directory.'
elif stat.S_ISLNK ( fileSTats [ stat.ST_MODe ] ):
  print 'Shortcut.'
elif stat.S_ISSOCK ( fileSTats [ stat.ST_MODe ] ):
  print 'Socket.'
elif stat.S_ISFIFO ( fileSTats [ stat.ST_MODe ] ):
  print 'Named pipe.'
elif stat.S_ISBLK ( fileSTats [ stat.ST_MODe ] ):
  print 'Block special device.'
elif stat.S_ISCHR ( fileSTats [ stat.ST_MODe ] ):
  print 'Character special device.'
```

Moreover, you can gather basic information using the 'os.path' as follows:

```
import os.path
fileStats = 'test.txt'
if os.path.isdir ( fileStats ):
  print 'Directory.'
elif os.path.isfile ( fileStats ):
  print 'File.'
elif os.path.islink ( fileStats ):
  print 'Shortcut.'
elif os.path.ismount ( fileStats ):
  print 'Mount point.'
{mospagebreak title=Directories}
```

Just like regular files, it is easy to work with directories. We will start by listing some directory's contents:

```
import os
for fileName in os.listdir ( '/' ):
  print fileName
```

You can see that this is very simple and you can do it in three lines.

Likewise, it is also simple to create a directory:

```
import os
os.mkdir ( 'testDirectory' )
```

It is also very easy to delete the directory you have created:

```
import os
os.rmdir ( 'testDirectory )
```

Creating multiple directories at a time is also easy to do:

```
import os
os.makedirs ( 'I/will/show/you/how/deep/the/rabbit/hole/goes'
)
```

Suppose you add nothing to the directories you have just created; it is also possible to delete them at once as follows:

```
import os
os.removedirs (
'I/will/show/you/how/deep/the/rabbit/hole/goes' )
```

Assume you want to do a particular action when the system reaches a certain type of file. You can do this easily using the module 'fnmatch'. Let us try printing all the contents the '.txt' files you come across and also print the filename of whichever '.exe' files you come across:

```
import fnmatch

import os

for fileName in os.listdir ( '/' ):

   if fnmatch.fnmath ( fileName, '*.txt' ):

     print open ( fileName ).read()

   elif fnmatch.fnmatch ( fileName, '*.exe' ):

     print fileName
```

The asterisk character can actually be representing any quantity of characters. If you want to match only a single character, you can simply use the question mark.

```
import fnmatch

import os

for fileName in os.listdir ( '/' ):

   if fnmatch.fnmatch ( fileName, '?.txt' ):

     print 'Text file.'
```

You can also try creating a regular expression with the module 'fnmatch', matching the filenames using the module 're' as follows:

```
import fnmatch
import os
import re
filePattern = fnmatch.translate ( '*.txt' )
for fileName in os.listdir ( '/' ):
  if re.match ( filePattern, fileName ):
    print 'Text file.'
```

If you are only searching for one filename type, it is a lot easier to use the module 'glob' as its patterns are just the same as those used in 'fnmatch':

```
import glob
for fileName in glob.glob ( '*.txt' ):
  print 'Text file.'
```

You can also use ranges of characters in the patterns in the same way as you would in regular expressions. Assume you desire to print the names of text files using a single digit right before the extension:

```
import glob
for fileName in glob.glob ( '[0-9].txt' ):
  print fileName
```

The "glob" module makes use of the "fnmatch" module.

{mospagebreak title=Pickling Data}

You can read strings from files and write them (the strings) to files with the methods we have seen in the previous section. Nonetheless, in a number of cases, you will find that you may have to pass the other data types like tuples, lists, dictionaries, among other objects.

In Python, this is possible using a method called pickling. The module 'pickle' contained in the standard library is what we use to pickle data. In this regard, we will begin by pickling a short list of integers and strings as follows:

```
import pickle

fileHandle = open ( 'pickleFile.txt', 'w' )

testList = [ 'This', 2, 'is', 1, 'a', 0, 'test.' ]

pickle.dump ( testList, fileHandle )

fileHandle.close()
```

Unpickling the data is just as easy:

```
import pickle

fileHandle = open ( 'pickleFile.txt' )

testList = pickle.load ( fileHandle )

fileHandle.does()
```

We can also store more complex data:

```
import pickle

fileHandle = open ( 'pickleFile.txt', 'w' )

testList = [ 123, { 'Calories' : 190 }, 'Mr. Anderson', [ 1, 2, 7] ]

pickle.dump ( testList, fileHandle )

fileHandle.close()
```

```
import pickle

fileHandle = open ( 'pickleFile.txt' )

testList = pickle.load ( fileHandle )

fileHandle.close()
```

With the example above, it is clear that pickling is a very easy to do with the pickle module in Python. Many objects may have it in their files. In addition, if the 'cPickle module' is available to you, you can also use it since it is exactly similar to the 'pickle' module, only faster. Here is how this looks:

```
import cPickle

fileHandle = open ( 'pickleFile.txt', 'w' )

cPickle.dump ( 1776, fileHandle )

fileHandle.close()

{mospagebreak title=Creating In-memory Files}
```

You will come across a number of modules that have methods that need a file object as an agreement. At times, creating and using a real file is inconvenient. Luckily, you can the module 'StringIO' to build files that store themselves in the memory of a computer:

```
import StringIO

fileHandle = StringIO.StringIO ( "Let freedom ring." )

print fileHandle.read() # "Let freedom ring."

fileHandle.close()
```

273

A "cStringIO" module is also availible. It is identical to the "StringIO" module in use, but, just like the "cPickle" module is to the "pickle" module, it is faster:

import cStringIO

fileHandle = cStringIO.cStringIO ("To Kill a Mockingbird")

print fileHandle.read() # "To Kill a Mockingbid"

fileHandle.close()

That is cool, is it not?

File management is a task you will come across as you practice programming because programmers using the different languages available today often encounter it on a daily basis.

Being a Python programmer, one of the greatest advantages you have is the fact that Python makes this task extremely simple when you compare the same to other languages. Python has a standard library that provides numerous modules that in turn come as a great help to you, the programmer. The fact that Python is object orientated also simplifies things further.

I am confident you now have a basic understanding of file management and that in future, you can use it in numerous Python applications.

In Python, we have numerous aspects that appeal to mathematicians. To mention but a few, we have in-built support meant for tuples, sets and lists, all of which have notation, which is pretty much the similar to that of list comprehensions and conventional mathematical notation, which are in turn very comparable to set comprehension as well as the set-builder notation that is used for them.

In Python, we also have another set of different features, which are very appealing to mathematicians. These are generators, iterators, and the 'itertools' package. With these tools, it is easy to write elegant code related to mathematical objects such as stochastic processes, infinite sequences, combinational structures, and recurrence relations.

Having noted that, the chapter of this book will thus take an in-depth look at iterators and generators.

Iterators in Python

Iterators are objects that permit iteration over a collection. These collections do not necessarily have to be of objects already existent in memory, and because of this, they also do not need to be finite.

Just to be more precise with our definition, you can say that an iterable is an object containing a '__inter__' method needed in returning an iterator object. On the other hand, an iterator is an object containing the '__inter__' method and '__next__' or just 'next'. In this case, the former returns an iterator object while the latter returns the subsequent element of the iteration. If you ask me, iterators are always returning 'self' in their '__inter__' method because they are simply their own iterators.

You should generally try to avoid calling 'next' and __inter__ directly. Python will call them for you automatically if you use list or 'for' comprehensions. In case you manually need to call them, you can use the built-in functions 'next' and 'inter' in Python and then pass the container or iterator as parameter. For instance, if 'c' happens to be an iterable, you can use 'inter(c)' rather than 'c.__inter__ ()'. Likewise, if 'a' happens to be an iterator, you can use 'next (a)' rather than 'a.next ()'. This is just the same as the use of 'len'.

Now that I mentioned it ('len'), you need to note that iterators do not have to have a properly defined length—and do not often have it anyway. This therefore means that they do not often implement '__len__'. In case you want to count the number of items present in an iterator, you need to do that manually or just use 'sum'.

Some iterables contain other objects, which serve as their iterators, and are thus not iterators themselves. For instance, the object 'list' is an iterable but not at all an iterator (instead of implementing 'next', it implements '__inter__'). As you can see in the example given below, iterators for the 'list' objects are of the 'listiterator' type. You may also notice how the 'list' objects contained a properly defined length; the listiterator objects do not have that.

```
>>> a = [1, 2]
>>> type(a)
<type 'list'>
>>> type(iter(a))
<type 'listiterator'>
>>> it = iter(a)
>>> next(it)
1
>>> next(it)
2
>>> next(it)
Traceback (most recent call last):
  File "<stdin>", line 1, in <module>
StopIteration
>>> len(a)
2
>>> len(it)
Traceback (most recent call last):
  File "<stdin>", line 1, in <module>
TypeError: object of type 'listiterator' has no len()
```

When an iterator completes, the interpreter expects it to raise the exception 'StopIteration'. Nonetheless, as mentioned, iterators can iterate over an endless set. Such kinds of iterators dictate that it is the responsibility of the user to make sure their use is not leading to an infinite loop. The example I will give in a bit will help you see what we mean by this.

The example I have given below shows a very basic case of an iterator. This iterator will just start counting at 0 and indeterminately rise. It is a version of 'itertools.count', only simpler.

```
class count_iterator(object):
  n = 0

  def __iter__(self):
    return self

  def next(self):
    y = self.n
    self.n += 1
    return y
```

The example below describes the usage. You need to note that the last line is trying to change the iterator object to a list, which ends up in an endless loop because the specific iterator does not end, ever.

```
>>> counter = count_iterator()
>>> next(counter)
0
>>> next(counter)
1
>>> next(counter)
2
>>> next(counter)
3
>>> list(counter) # This will result in an infinite loop!
```

Lastly, just to be accurate, you have to amend the above example. The objects that lack a well-defined method '__inter__' may still be iterable, that is, if they define '__getitem__'. In this case, Python's built-in function 'iter' returns an iterator of 'iterator' type for the object that uses '__getitem__' to go through the list's items. If '__getitem__' raises either 'IndexError' or 'StopIteration' the iteration subsequently stops. The example of this is below:

```
class SimpleList(object):
    def __init__(self, *items):
        self.items = items

    def __getitem__(self, i):
        return self.items[i]
```

And its use:

```
>>> a = SimpleList(1, 2, 3)
>>> it = iter(a)
>>> next(it)
1
>>> next(it)
2
>>> next(it)
3
>>> next(it)
Traceback (most recent call last):
  File "<stdin>", line 1, in <module>
StopIteration
```

To make things a bit more interesting, we can now look at another example: creating the Hofstadter Q sequence using an iterator given the initial conditions. First mention of this nested recurrence was by Hofstadter in a book called "An Eternal Golden Braid." Ever since, the issue of demonstrating that the sequence is properly defined for the 'n' values has been open. Look at the code below that uses an iterator to create a sequence provided by the nested recurrence.

$$Q(n)=Q(n- Q(n- 1))+Q(n- Q(n- 2))$$

Given the initial conditions, for instance, 'qsequence([1, 1])', will create the same exact Hofstadter sequence. We use the exception 'StopIteration' to indicate that the sequence cannot go anymore because there is need for an invalid index to generate the subsequent element. For instance, if [1,2] are the initial conditions, the sequence will immediately 'terminate'.

```
class qsequence(object):
    def __init__(self, s):
        self.s = s[:]

    def next(self):
        try:
            q = self.s[-self.s[-1]] + self.s[-self.s[-2]]
            self.s.append(q)
            return q
        except IndexError:
            raise StopIteration()

    def __iter__(self):
        return self

    def current_state(self):
        return self.s
```

You can use it like so:

```
>>> Q = qsequence([1, 1])
>>> next(Q)
2
>>> next(Q)
3
>>> [next(Q) for __ in xrange(10)]
[3, 4, 5, 5, 6, 6, 6, 8, 8, 8]
```

NOTE: Iterators are greatly advantageous because they save resources. For instance, you could get all the odd numbers without having to store the whole number system in the memory. Theoretically, you can also have infinite items in finite memory. Besides that, you would agree that iterator makes code look cool.

Python Generators

Python generators are functions that create sequences of results. These generators maintain their local state to ensure that the function resumes where they left off whenever it has been called at any subsequent times. You can thus think of a generator as some sort of a powerful iterator.

The function state is maintained with the keyword when the 'yield' keyword is used, and contains the syntax below;

yield [expression_list]

In Python, this keyword works a lot like using 'return' but it has important differences that we shall explain throughout this chapter.

How Generators Work

To understand how generators work, we will look at a simple example:

```python
# generator_example_1.py

def numberGenerator(n):
    number = 0
    while number < n:
        yield number
        number += 1

myGenerator = numberGenerator(3)

print(next(myGenerator))
print(next(myGenerator))
print(next(myGenerator))
```

The above code is defining a generator with the name 'numberGenerator' that gets a value 'n' as the argument, before defining and using it in a while loop as the limit value. Additionally, it is defining a variable containing the name 'number' and assigning to it the zero value.

When you call the instantiated generator that is 'myGenerator' with the method 'next()', it runs the generator code until the initial 'yield' statement; and in this case, this is returning 1.

Even when the value returns to you, the function then tends to keep the variable 'number' value for when you call the function next and grows its value by one. Thus, it picks up exactly where it left off at the next call of the function. When you call the function two more times, you shall get the next two numbers in the sequence as you can see here:

```
$ python generator_example_1.py
0
1
2
```

If you were to call this generator once more, you would get an exception 'StopIteration' since it had finished and reverted from its internal while loop.

This is a useful functionality since you can dynamically use generators to create iterables as you go. If you were to use 'list()' to wrap 'myGenerator' you would get an array of numbers such as [0,1,2] back as opposed to a generator object; this is somewhat easier to work with when it comes to certain applications.

Let us now see the difference between yield and return.

The Difference between Yield and Between

The 'return' keyword usually returns a value from a given function and when this happens time, the function usually loses its local state. This therefore means that the next time you call that particular function, it starts afresh from its first statement.

Conversely, 'yield' keeps the state between the different function calls and then starts from where it had stopped when the method 'next()' is called again. Therefore, in case 'yield', is called in the generator, it means that you will pick right back up after the final 'yield' statement the next time this generator is called.

The Use of Return in a Generator

The generator can use the 'return' statement but only when there lacks a return value, which is in the form below:

```
return
```

The generator goes on as in any other function return when it gets the 'return' statement. The return simply means "I am done, and don't have anything interesting to return"; that is for generator functions as well as non-generator functions (according to the PEP 255).

We will now try to modify our previous example by including an if-else clause. This will discriminate against the numbers beyond 20. The code is:

```
# generator_example_2.py

def numberGenerator(n):
  if n < 20:
    number = 0
    while number < n:
      yield number
      number += 1
  else:
    return

print(list(numberGenerator(30)))
```

This example shows that the generator will be an empty array because it will not yield any values because 30 is higher than the number 20. In this case, the return statement works in the same way as the break statement. We can see this as follows:

```
$ python generator_example_2.py
[]
```

Loading...

In case you assigned a value below 20, the results would not have been any different from the first example.

The Use of next() In Iterating Through a Generator

Can you remember what we learnt about parsing? Well, as the first example describes, you can use the method 'next() to parse values yielded by a generator. This method informs the generator to return only the next iterable value, and nothing more. For instance, the code below prints the values from 0 to 9 on the screen.

```python
# generator_example_3.py

def numberGenerator(n):
    number = 0
    while number < n:
        yield number
        number += 1

g = numberGenerator(10)

counter = 0

while counter < 10:
    print(next(g))
    counter += 1
```

The code above is the same as the earlier ones with the only difference being that it calls every yielded value (by the generator) with the 'next()' function. To do this, you first have to instantiate a generator, which is just like a variable holding the generator state.

By calling the 'next()' function with the generator being its argument, the generator function in Python comes into play until a 'yield' statement is found. After that, the value yielded is returned to the caller before the state of the generator gets saved for later use used later.

When you run the code above, you will get the output below:

```
$ python generator_example_3.py
0
1
2
3
4
5
6
7
8
9
```

However, there is a difference of syntax between Python 3 and 2. The code you are seeing above is using Python 3. In Python 2, 'next()' can actually use the last syntax or the one below:

```
print(g.next())
```

Generator Expressions

Generator expressions are similar to the list comprehensions, only that instead of returning a list, they return a generator. These became part of Python since the 2.4 version but their proposal was in PEP 289.

The syntax for generator expressions is the same as list comprehension only that it uses parenthesis instead of square brackets.

For instance, we can modify the code we had before with generator expressions in the following manner:

```
# generator_example_4.py

g = (x for x in range(10))
print(list(g))
```

The results here are similar to what we had in the first few examples. Here is a look at that:

```
$ python generator_example_4.py
[0, 1, 2, 3, 4, 5, 6, 7, 8, 9]
```

The generator expressions come in handy when you are using reductions functions like 'max()', 'min()', or 'sum()' because they decrease the code to just a single line. You are also likely to find them being a lot shorter to type than the full generator function. As an example, the code below sums up the first ten numbers:

```
# generator_example_5.py

g = (x for x in range(10))
print(sum(g))
```

When you run the code, you will get the following result:

```
$ python generator_example_5.py
45
```

Managing Exceptions

Something important you have to note is the fact that the keyword 'yield' should not be in the 'try' part of a finally/try construct. This means generators ought to allocate resources with caution.

Nonetheless, you can find 'yield' appearing in clauses like 'except', 'finally' or in try/even clauses—that is in the 'try' part.

For instance, you could have made the code below:

```
# generator_example_6.py

def numberGenerator(n):
  try:
    number = 0
    while number < n:
      yield number
      number += 1
  finally:
    yield n

print(list(numberGenerator(10)))
```

In the above code, the number 10 is part of the output because of the clause 'finally' and the result is a number list beginning from 0 up to 10. This would not normally happen because 'number<n' is the conditional statement. We can see this in the following output:

```
$ python generator_example_6.py
[0, 1, 2, 3, 4, 5, 6, 7, 8, 9, 10]
```

Send Values to Generators

Generators have a powerful tool in the method 'send()' for generator-iterators. This method has been available since version 2.5 of Python but its definition was in PEP 342. The method 'send()' resumes the generator and then sends a value to be used to continue with the subsequent 'yield'. The method then returns the value yielded by the generator.

'send(value)' or 'send()' is the syntax. The send method is equal to a 'next()' call without any value. This method can also use 'None' as a value. In the two cases, the outcome is that the generator is advancing its execution to the initial 'yield' expression.

If the generator happens to exit without yielding a new value (such as using return), the method 'sand()' will raise 'StopIteration'.

The example below demonstrates the use of 'send()'. You will ask the program to assign the 'number' variable the value yielded before—that is in the first line and third line as well. After the generator function (that is in the first line), you instantiate the generator and then create a first 'yield' in the subsequent line by calling the 'next' function. Therefore, in the final line, you send the value 5, which the generator will use as input and taken as its previous yield.

```
# generator_example_7.py

def numberGenerator(n):
    number = yield
    while number < n:
        number = yield number
        number += 1

g = numberGenerator(10)   # Create our generator
next(g)               #
print(g.send(5))
```

Note that since there is no yielded value at the initial creation of the generator, you have to ensure the generator yielded a value (before using 'send()') using 'send(None)' or 'next()'. In the above example, you can execute the line 'next(g)' for this reason alone; in any case, the only other thing we would be getting is an error.

When you run the program, you will find that it prints the 5 as a value on the screen, which is exactly what we sent to it anyway.

```
$ python generator_example_7.py
5
```

Our generator's third line from above also shows a new feature in Python that introduced yield expressions (in the same PEP). This feature lets us use the 'yield' clause on the right side of an assignment statement. 'None' is the yield expression value, until the program calls the 'send(value)' method.

Connect the Generators

A new feature that become part of Python from version 3.3 lets generators connect themselves and also delegate to a sub-generator as well. Definition of this expression is in <u>PEP 380</u>. It has the following syntax:

```
yield from <expression>
```

Here, <expression> is just an expression that evaluates to an iterable defining the delegating generator.

The example below demonstrates this:

```
# generator_example_8.py

def myGenerator1(n):
    for i in range(n):
        yield i

def myGenerator2(n, m):
    for j in range(n, m):
        yield j

def myGenerator3(n, m):
    yield from myGenerator1(n)
    yield from myGenerator2(n, m)
    yield from myGenerator2(m, m+5)

print(list(myGenerator1(5)))
print(list(myGenerator2(5, 10)))
print(list(myGenerator3(0, 10)))
```

The above code defines three distinct generators. In this case, the first one with the name 'myGenerator1' contains an input parameter used to specify a range limit. The second one, called 'myGenerator2' is just the same as the former one but has two input parameters that specify the two limits permitted in the number range. 'myGenerator3' calls both 'myGenerator1' and 'myGenerator2' after this to yield their values.

The final three lines of the code usually print three lists on the screen. These lists are generated from the three previously defined generators. As you can see by running the program below, the product is that 'myGenerator' uses the yields acquired from 'myGenerator1' as well as 'myGenerator2' so that it generates a list combining the last three lists.

According to the example, we also see a significant application of generators, i.e. the ability to divide a lengthy task into a number of distinct sections that can be useful when working with large data sets.

```
$ python generator_example_8.py
[0, 1, 2, 3, 4]
[5, 6, 7, 8, 9]
[0, 1, 2, 3, 4, 5, 6, 7, 8, 9, 10, 11, 12, 13, 14]
```

You can see that thanks to the syntax 'yield from', you can chain together generators to have a more dynamic programming.

Benefits of Generators

What are the benefits of generators? You might ask...

For one, they simplify code. As you can see in the examples we looked at in this chapter, generators make code simple and elegant. The elegance and code simplification becomes even more apparent in generator expressions where a given line of code actually becomes a replacement for a whole block of code.

Secondly, generators offer better performance. In this regard, they work on the on-demand (or lazy) generation of values.

Two advantages come out of this: first, we get lower consumption of memory. This 'memory saving' works to our benefit only if we use the generator just once. In cases where we use values severally, it may be important to generate them all at once and keep them for use later.

The fact that generators possess an 'on-demand' nature means you may not necessarily have to create values that have no use. This would cause wasted cycles in case their generation happened. This therefore means your program only has to use the required values without having to wait for the generation of each one of them.

When to Use Generators

As we have seen, generators are some of the most advanced tools contained in Python. In programming, we do have several cases where generators can improve efficiency. Some of these include the following:

- When you want to process tons of data; in this case, generators offer calculation on-demand, which some people like calling lazy evaluation. This method is very common in stream processing.

- Secondly, you can use stacked generators in piping—as pipes. This is in the same way as in UNIX pipes. Put differently, you can use generators to pipeline a series of operations. Here is an example explaining this: Say you have a log file from a renowned food chain. This log file contains a column (the fourth column) that follows up on the number of pizzas sold per hour and you want to sum it to get the total number of pizzas the food chain has sold in five years. Suppose everything is in a string and the non-available numbers are labelled as 'N/A'.

The following code represents a good generator implementation of all this.

```
with open('sells.log') as file:
  pizza_col = (line[3] for line in file)
  per_hour = (int(x) for x in pizza_col if x != 'N/A')
  print("Total pizzas sold = ",sum(per_hour))
```

This is an example of an efficient pipeline that is simple to read and so much cooler; is that not so?

Finally, you can use generators in concurrency to generate or simulate concurrency (read more on concurrency).

Take Away DIY Example: The Eratosthenes Sieve

There once lived an Alexandrian mathematician called Eratosthenes of Cyrene. He invented a great notion for filtering out prime numbers.

Here is how it works:

Assume you want to know all the prime numbers below a number such as 1000. First, you cancel all the multiples of two from a list (except 2) 1...1000. You will now cancel all the multiples of 3 apart from 3. 4, being a multiple of 2, has been cancelled already. You will now take off the entire multiples of 5 apart from 5 and so forth. Eventually, what you will remain in your list are the prime numbers.

Let us begin with a generator that gives you all the integers from i moving upwards.

```
def intsfrom(i):
      while 1:
            yield i
          i = i + 1
```

We will now write a generator that eliminates all multiples of a number 'n' from a sequence as follows:

```
def exclude_multiples(n, ints):
        for i in ints:
                if (i % n):
                        yield i
```

Invoking a generator, for instance, list(firstn(exclude_multiples(2, intsfrom(1)), 5)), gives you a list of [1,3,5,79].

It is now time to build your 'sieve'.

```
def sieve(ints):
        while 1:
                prime = ints.next()
                yield prime
                ints = exclude_multiples(prime, ints)
```

If you want the source file that contains these function definitions, see the code below:

```
from __future__ import generators

def firstn(g, n):
        for i in range(n):
                yield g.next()

def intsfrom(i):
        while 1:
                yield i
                i = i + 1

def exclude_multiples(n, ints):
        for i in ints:
                if (i % n): yield i
```

PYTHON PROGRAMMING FOR ADVANCED

```python
def sieve(ints):
    while 1:
        prime = ints.next()
        yield prime
        ints = exclude_multiples(prime, ints)

if __name__ == '__main__':
    for i in firstn(sieve(intsfrom(2)), 400):
        print i
```

Intertools in Python

Intertools is one of the coolest thing in Python. Even though it contains an elusively technical name and a reduced emphasis in most introductory materials in Python, Intertools is the type of built-in package that works to make list comprehensions a lot less of a syntactical mess.

You will find that the biggest barrier to the use of Intertools is that Python has many methods that more or less perform similar tasks. Having said that, this mini-chapter is a simple showcase of a bit of the rather basic but still rad stuff you could use these methods to do.

First things first

We will begin by getting the boring section out of the way:

```
import itertools

letters = ['a', 'b', 'c', 'd', 'e', 'f']
booleans = [1, 0, 1, 0, 0, 1]
numbers = [23, 20, 44, 32, 7, 12]
decimals = [0.1, 0.7, 0.4, 0.4, 0.5]
```

That was easy, was it not?

Chain()

This method does what you would want it to do i.e. you provide a list of tuples/iterables/lists, and it joins them for you. I am sure you have not forgotten how, as a child, you used tape to join paper. This is pretty much the same thing with the only difference being that it is in Python. Let us try doing it!

print itertools.chain(letters, booleans, decimals)

>>> <itertools.chain object at 0x2c7ff0>

Do not worry about what happened. In intertools, the inter represents iterable, which you already know about. You know that printing iterables is not what you would call the most difficult thing in Python because you only need to have it cast to a list as follows:

print list(itertools.chain(letters, booleans, decimals))

>>> ['a', 'b', 'c', 'd', 'e', 'f', 1, 0, 1, 0, 0, 1, 0.1, 0.7, 0.4, 0.4, 0.5]

That is a lot better! Chain() works also as you would imagine, with iterables/lists of varying lengths as follows:

print list(itertools.chain(letters, letters[3:]))

>>> ['a', 'b', 'c', 'd', 'e', 'f', 'd', 'e', 'f']

Do not worry if you come across most of the methods surrounded with list() casts because I think that is necessary for purposes of making this section readable.

Count()

Suppose you want to conduct a sensitivity analysis of a very important business simulation. The very important business simulation we are talking about revolves around the hopes that on average, the cost of a widget is ten dollars, but in a couple of months, the demand for that widget could explode over the subsequent months and you want to ensure you will not hemorrhage cash if it costs more. You thus want a list of theoretical widget costs passing to 'magic_business_ simulation()'

With list comprehensions playing a part, it could look something like so:

[(i * 0.25) + 10 for i in range(100)]

>>> [10.0, 10.25, 10.5, 10.75, ...]

This is actually not bad at all, save for the fact that reading it is hard, particularly if you are chaining that list comprehension within another list comprehension. With intertools, it could look something like this:

itertools.count(10, 0.25)

I hope you are feeling good about yourself so far and maybe thinking how the function you pass a starting point and step size knows when to stop.

The answer to that is simple: it never stops. Just like many other methods, intertools generates infinitely until you abort through something like break. You also need to note that intertools is much about iterables; you know that infinite iterables could be scary right now but they will be so helpful as you move ahead.

Therefore, you can say that you only want the values of the method above up until twenty dollars— apparently, this widget has a very elastic demand. How do you then cut off 'count()'? I will give you a hint—some other intertools function.

Ifilter()

This method is an easy invocation of a simple user case below:

298

```
print list(itertools.ifilter(lambda x: x % 2, numbers))
```

```
>>> [23, 7]
```

I think you can see how simple that is. We pass in a function as well as an iterable object, which returns a list of the objects that evaluate true when passed into the function. Therefore, in order to solve the small widget problem from before:

```
print list(itertools.ifilter(lambda x: x < 20, itertools.count(10,
0.25))
```

```
>>> ...
```

```
>>> ...
```

Well, that will still go on infinitely since count() will continue bringing values. Moreover, even though they will still be ignored by 'ifilter()', it has to process them. Therefore, how can we do this? A common pattern is:

```
for i in itertools.count(10, 0.25):
  if i < 20:
    do_something()
  else:
    break
```

This is quite readable:

Compress()

This method is what most programmers use. Many consider it perfect: two lists given (a and b) return the 'a' elements and the corresponding elements of 'b' for it ('a') are true.

```
print list(itertools.compress(letters, booleans))
```

```
>>> ['a', 'c', 'f']
```

Imap()

This is the last method we will discuss as a simple addition for those who are presumably already versed in the functional programming stapes of 'filter' and 'map': 'map()' is simply a map version that creates an iterable. When you pass it a function, it grabs arguments systematically and throws them at the function to return the results:

print list(itertools.imap(mult, numbers, decimals))

> [2.2, 14.0, 17.6, 12.8, 3.5]

Maybe you would consider using 'None' in lieu of a function to have back the iterables grouped as tuples.

print list(itertools.imap(None, numbers, decimals))

> [(22, 0.1), (20, 0.7), (44, 0.4), (32, 0.4), (7, 0.5)]

If you ask me, these are the five most important intertools elements. There are, however, many more. For now, just try playing around with the ones we have discussed before looking for others. These methods are awesome by themselves but it will benefit you to save a couple of lines and characters by moving away from list comprehensions—that pales when you compare it to what you can achieve when you combine the methods together.

You can find many great examples highlighting the power of intertools when paired with intertools. As a take-out, look at one of the best ones below:

```python
def unique_everseen(utterable, key=None):
"List unique elements, preserving order. Remember all element
ever seen."
# unique_everseen('AAAABBBCCDAABBB') --> A B C D
# unique_everseen('ABBCcAD', str.lower) --> A B C D
seen = set()
seen_add = seen.add
if key is None:
   for element in ifilterfalse(seen.__contains__, utterable):
      seen_add(element)
      yield element
else:
   for element in utterable:
      k = key(element)
      if k not in seen:
         seen_add(k)
         yield element
```

Closures in Python

Closures are exciting Python functions. A closure is a Python function that allows you to do things you would otherwise not achieve with functions in other popular languages such as Java C or C ++.

Python treats everything a lot like as a 'first-class citizen' so you can pass them around as some normal variables. The same applies for functions. At this level, I expect you have already seen code like the one below:

```
>>> def adder(a, b):
...     return a + b
...
>>> def caller(fun):
...     print(fun(2, 4))
...     print(fun(3, 5))
...
>>> caller(adder)
6
8
```

The example you are seeing above made a function caller that calls a different function passed to it as an argument.

Since you can pass functions around as arguments, you can as well return functions from the function calls. Take the example below:

```
>>> def contains_factory(x):
...     def contains(lst):
...         return x in lst
...     return contains
...
>>> contains_15 = contains_factory(15)
```

When you run this example, the 'contains_15' has the function type:

```
<function contains_factory.<locals>.contains at 0x101d78b70>
```

The functions here are closures.

Why Closures are Considered Special in Python

If so far you are thinking that closures are ordinary functions, you may have missed the main difference from the former example.

Call 'contains_15' with some iterables or lists to have the functionality tested:

```
>>> contains_15([1,2,3,4,5])
False
>>> contains_15([13, 14, 15, 16, 17])
True
>>> contains_15(range(1, 20))
True
```

What you need to note is that closures remember the context in which they were made. The example above 'contains_15' does remember that the function 'contains_factory' was called with value 15. This 15, moreover, is used for later in the function 'contains' as the x variable when you give many iterables so that they look up x in them.

Apart from that, you might want to know that the closure stays existing even when the original creator function – which is 'contains_factory' in the example–is deleted:

```
>>> del contains_factory
>>> contains_factory(42)
Traceback (most recent call last):
  File "<stdin>", line 1, in <module>
NameError: name 'contains_factory' is not defined
>>> contains_15(range(14, 20))
True
```

How to Build a Closure

Well, this might seem like a reiteration because by this time, you should already know how to build closures in Python. Do not worry though because I will sum things up for the sake of brevity:

You have to create a nested function–that is, a function within another function.

The nested function has to refer or allude to a variable defined within the enclosing function.

The enclosing function needs to return the nested function.

I bet you found that very simple!

The second part is simple and optional—if you however fail to have a variable referenced from the enclosing function, you will not find a lot of sense in creating a nested function and returning it—you just define a function. You can do this in the normal scope as well.

Let us try creating another exciting closure—that is, a counter. The main idea behind this (counter) is that in certain cases, you simply want to count interactions. In such cases, you define a global variable—usually known as counter—and increase (increment) it at the right place when there is an interaction occurring. You can have this global variable replaced as well as the incrementation each time you desire to count something.

```
>>> def counter_factory():
...    count = 0 # here I create the variable to increment
...    def counter():
...        nonlocal count
...        count += 1
...        return count
...    return counter
...
```

As you can see in the example above, a function to generate a counter closure as it gets invoked each time has been created, and the counter begins from zero and increases each time the closure is called.

```
>>> counter1 = counter_factory()
>>> counter1()
1
>>> counter1()
2
>>> counter2 = counter_factory()
>>> counter2()
1
>>> counter1()
3
>>> counter2()
2
```

This solution is not exactly what you want because with the invocation of the function, you return the value of count each time. This simply means that if you want to verify that there were no interactions, you would have to do something such as:

counter1() == 1

This actually requires some remembering and thinking as well—but we are human beings who make errors.

Lucky for you, we have a solution for that. An enclosing function does not have any special limits on the number of closures returned. Therefore, fixing this issue requires creating two closures, one of them will result to increment in the count variable as the other returns the present value of the count variable as follows:

```
>>> def counter_factory():
...     count = 0 # here I create the variable
...     def counter():
...         nonlocal count
...         count += 1
...         return count
...     def current():
...         nonlocal count
...         return count
...     return (counter, current)
```

You now have to access the two closures and you can use them as you wish:

```
>>> incrementer, getter = counter_factory()
>>> getter
<function counter_factory.<locals>.current at 0x102478bf8>
>>> incrementer
<function counter_factory.<locals>.counter at 0x1024789d8>
>>> getter()
0
>>> getter()
0
>>> incrementer()
>>> incrementer()
>>> incrementer()
>>> getter()
3
>>> getter()
3
>>> incrementer()
>>> getter()
```

```
4
>>> incrementer, getter = counter_factory()
>>> getter()
0
>>> incrementer()
>>> getter()
1
```

As you can see, the incrementer silently increments the count value within the closure. 'getter' returns the definite value of count and yet it does not increment it; this makes the feature very usable. You can reset the counter by re-assigning the closures.

Uses of Closure

With that said, what do you think closures are good for?

Even though closures might appear to be very interesting, another question is apparent. Where can you use closures in order to put them to their best use? Well, in summary, you can use them to:

✓ Eliminate global variables

✓ Replace hard-coded constants

✓ Provide signatures for consistent functions

Late Closure Binding

The manner in which Python usually binds the different variables in closures is a source of problem. For instance, you write the following:

```
>>> def create_adders():
...     adders = []
...     for i in range(10):
...         def adder(x):
...             return i + x
...         adders.append(adder)
...     return adders
...
>>> for adder in create_adders():
...     print(adder(1))
...
```

You may expect the output below:

```
2
3
4
5
6
7
8
9
10
11
```

In reality, you get this:

```
10
10
10
10
10
10
10
10
10
10
```

What happens? You build ten functions that include 1 to the number 9. This happens because of the closures' late binding.

The variables used within the closures are looked up as soon as the inner function is called. Each time the adder function is called, you will find that the inner loop that is over the 'range(10)' is complete and the i variable contains the value 9. This means that you will end up with 10 for every ten functions in consequence.

To solve this problem, you will thus have to add another parameter to your closures; this will maintain the proper state:

```
>>> def create_adders():
...    adders = []
...    for i in range(10):
...        def adder(x, i=i):
...            return i + x
...        adders.append(adder)
...    return adders
```

In this case, you added to the closure i as a local variable with a default i value. This then comes from the range and then sets the closure value i then to 0 and then 9 in that order. Running the example will solve the problem for you:

```
>>> for adder in create_adders():
...    print(adder(1))
...
1
2
3
4
5
6
7
8
9
10
```

Well, that is all you need to know today on closures. You have seen that closures are simply functions that remember the lexical scope or context they were created in and can use it even when the program flow is not in the enclosing scope anymore.

If you want to create a closure such that the returned function becomes the closure itself, you can write a function that returns another function.

Finally, you have learned that variables are essentially late binding. This means you have to take care when using them as you can easily end up with undesirable results.

Regular Expressions (RE) In Python

This chapter presents to you a comprehensive and detailed introduction to Python's regular expressions. After reading this chapter, you should be able to explain regular expressions' theoretical aspects and know how to utilize them in the Python scripts.

Sometimes, the term 'regular expressions' are known as regexp or regex and have their roots in theoretical computer science. In this branch, we use them to make definitions of a language family with particular characteristics also known as regular languages. Finite state machines (FSMs) that accept regular expression-defined language exists for all regular expressions.

In programming languages, we use regular expressions to filter texts/textsrings and it is possible to see whether a string or text is matching a regular expression.

You also need to note another aspect of regular expressions that is equally important: the regular expressions' syntax does not change in any programming languages and script languages such as Java, Python, AWK, Perl, SED, or even X#.

Well, let us begin.

In the first 'beginners' edition of this Python programming series, you learned a bit about sequential data types, specifically about the operator 'in'. In the example below, check to see whether the string easily is indeed a substring of 'regular expressions easily explained' which itself is a string.

```
>>> s = "Regular expressions easily explained!"
>>> "easily" in s
True
>>>
```

The diagrams below are systematically showing how we do this matching. You check whether the string sub= abc is located inside the string s= 'xaababcbcd' as shown in the diagram.

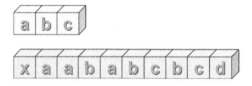

As a matter of fact, the sub= 'abc' string can be seen as a regular expression—only a very simple one. In the first place, you check whether the first positions of both strings are matching- that is s[0] == sub[0]. In your example here, this is not the case. You thus mark this fact with red color:

After that, you go on to check whether s[1:4] == sub. This means you first have to check whether sub[0] is equivalent to s[1]. This being true, you use the green color to mark it. You then have to compare the subsequent positions. The s[2] is not an equivalent of sub[1] and thus, you do not have to go on further with the next sub and s position.

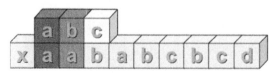

At this point, you have to check whether sub and s[2:5] are equal. Both first positions are equal, but this does not apply to the third:

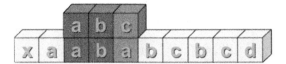

The steps below have to be clear devoid of any explanations:

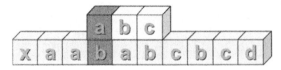

Lastly, you have yourself a complete match —that is with s[4:7] == sub:

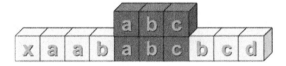

From what we have discussed, you already know that you can see the 'sub' variable as a very simple expression. In Python, using regular expressions means you have to import the re module, which essentially offers functions and methods of dealing with regular expressions.

Python's Representation of Regular Expressions

If you have used other programming languages, you know that representing regular expressions inside slashes is the order of the day —"/" and that is the way AWK, Perl, or SED deals with them. In Python however, there are no special notations. The regular expressions are simply represented as normal strings, which as you can guess, is very convenient. Even so, this carries a little problem.

The backslash is a special character used in regular expressions, but also used in strings as an escape character. This shows that Python would firstly evaluate all string backslashes and only after this—that is without the necessary backslashes—would it take it as a regular expression.

A good way to prevent this would be writing every backlash in the form: "\\" so that you reserve it for the regular expression's evaluation. The best approach to deal with the problem is by marking the regular expressions as what's referred to as 'raw strings'.

r"^a.*\.html$"

The regular example we saw in the earlier example does match all file names or strings that begin with the letter 'a' and end with the word 'html'. You will understand this more as we move ahead further—that is the structure of the above example.

The Syntax of Regular Expressions

Simple as it is, r"cat" is an example of a regular expression even though it does not have any metacharacters. The regular expression r"cat" matches, for instance, the string below:

"A rat and cat cannot be friends."

Interestingly though, the previous example is already showing a 'favorite' mistake example commonly made by beginners, novices, and sometimes even advanced users of RE.

In this example, the main idea is matching strings that have the word "cat." Unfortunately, while we are successful with that, we are also matching many other words. It might still be fine to match 'cats' in a string but you need to ask yourself what will happen to the rest of the words that contain this 'cat' character sequence. You can match words such as 'communicate', 'education', 'ramifications', 'falsification', 'cattle' among many others. This case is showing overmatching where you get positive results that, according to the problem you are looking to solve, are wrong.

The diagram above illustrates this problem properly. The circle 'C' with a shade of dark green corresponds to the category or group of 'objects' you want to recognize. However, you match all elements of 'O' where we have the blue circle instead. C is therefore a subset of O.

Again, in the diagram, the circle in light green 'U' is a subset of C. In this case, U is an issue of 'under matching'- that is, if the regular expression does not match all the intended strings. When you try fixing the previous regular expression so that you keep it from creating over matching, you could try the r" cat " expression. The blanks here keep the matching of the words mentioned above such as 'falsification', 'education' and 'ramification' from matching. Still, you may fall prey to yet another mistake.

Consider the string 'The cat, named Oscar, climbed on the tree.' The issue here is that we are not expecting a comma, only a blank behind the name 'cat'.

Just before we proceed with describing the syntax of regular expressions, we will first have to explain how you can use them in Python:

```
>>> import re
>>> x = re.search("cat","A cat and a rat can't be friends.")
>>> print x
<_sre.SRE_Match object at 0x7fd4bf238238>
>>> x = re.search("cow","A cat and a rat can't be friends.")
>>> print x
None
```

In the last example, you had to import the re module so that you can work with regular expressions. You then used the search method from the module re. This could this module's most important and most common method.

re.serch(expr,s) is meant to check a string 's' for a substring occurrence that matches the expr regular expression. The initial substring—from the left side—satisfying this condition will be returned. If a match has been made possible, we consequently receive a match object; otherwise, we get the none value. This method is enough to use regular expressions already in the Python programs:

```
>>> if re.search("cat","A cat and a rat can't be friends."):
...    print "Some kind of cat has been found :-)"
... else:
...    print "No cat has been found :-("
...
Some kind of cat has been found :-)
>>> if re.search("cow","A cat and a rat can't be friends."):
...    print "Cats and Rats and a cow."
... else:
...    print "No cow around."
...
No cow around.
```

Any Character

We will now suppose that the previous example has not interested you in recognizing the word cat but rather, all the three letter words ending with 'at'. The regular expressions' syntax supplies "." , a metacharacter used for 'any character' like a placeholder. In our example, we can write the regular expression like so:

```
r" .at "
```

In this case, the regular expression matches three letter words, separated by blanks, ending in 'at'. We will now get words such as 'cat', 'eat', 'rat', 'bat', 'sat' among many more. Even so, what if the text has words such as '3at' or something like '@at'? These words are matching as well, which means you have created over matching again. The solution lies in the next section.

Character Classes

We use square brackets "]" and "[" to take in a character class. For instance, [xyz] means either 'x', 'y' or a 'z'. To understand what this means practically, look at the example below:

r"M[ae][iy]er"

What you are seeing is a regular expression that matches a common surname in German, a name containing four different spellings but the same pronunciation: Meyer, Maier, Meier, and Mayer.

The following diagram shows a finite state automata(automaton) —also called a finite state machine (FSM), a computation model that you can implement with software or hardware to use in a desired way like simulating

317

some computer programs as well as sequential logic]—that we can build to recognize this expression.

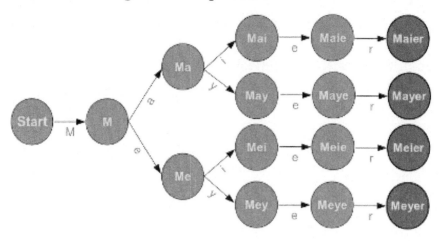

The finite state machine graph is simple so that the design remains easy. In the start node, there should be an arrow pointing back on its own—that is, in the instance a character apart from an upper case 'M' becomes processed, the machine has to remain in the start condition.

Additionally, there should be an arrow that points back from the various final nodes (see the ones in green) to the start node; otherwise, the letter expected has been processed. For instance, if the machine is currently in state Ma once it has processed 'M' and 'a', it (the machine) has to return to 'start' state if any character other than 'y' or 'i' can be read. Well, if you are having problems with this FSM, you should not worry since having a full grasp of it is not necessary for what we are going to discuss next or in this book.

Rather than making a choice between two characters, you may often have to choose between the larger character classes. For instance, you could need a class of letters running from 'a' and 'e' or maybe between 'o' and '5'. In order to manage these character classes, the regular expressions' syntax supplies "-", a metacharacter. [a-e] being an easy writing for this [abcde] or [012345] denoted by [0-5].

The advantage here is obvious and actually more impressive. Rather than having, for instance, [ABCDEFGHIJKLMNOPQRSTUVWXYZ], you can just write [A-Z]. If you do not find this convincing, just write 'any lower case or uppercase letter'- an expression for the character class [A-Za-z].

Well, there is a bit more you need to know about the dash (you used to mark the start and end of a character class). The dash only takes a special meaning if you use it within square brackets, and in this case, if you place it in front of a closing bracket or directly after the opening of the same.

Therefore, an expression like [-az is only the choice among the three characters including 'a', '-' and 'z' and no other characters. This is also true for [az-.

Let us see if you understood anything. Try the following exercise:

Which is the character class being described by [-a-z]?

What is your answer?

The answer is simple: the '-' and the entire list of characters 'a', b'', 'c'...all the way to 'z'.

The caret "^" is the only other special character within square brackets (the character class choice). It negates the choice if you tend to use it directly after an opening square bracket. 'any character but not a digit' is denoted by [^0-9]. The caret position within the square brackets is important. It contains no special meaning unless you position it as the first character after the opening square bracket.

Anything but an 'a', 'b' or 'c' is denoted by [^abc]

An 'a', 'b', 'c' or 'a' "^" is denoted by [a^bc]

Practical Exercise

Before we proceed with our chapter on regular expressions, let us try to have a practical exercise:

You know the famous Simpsons (an American animated TV series). Well, you have their phone list. We have some people who have Neu as their surname. You are looking for a Neu; you do not know the first name but you know it starts with a J. You will write a Python script that finds all the lines of the phonebook that contains the person having the described surname as well as a first name that begins with J. In case you do not know how to read and work with files, you can go back to the first chapter on file management. A good example script can be as follows:

```
import re

fh = open("simpsons_phone_book.txt"
for line in fh:
    if re.search(r"J.*Neu",line):
        print line.rstrip()
fh.close()
```

Repetitions

Sometimes in programming, you will get tired trying to find long patterns in sequences. Lucky for you though, the module 're' can handle repetitions with the special characters below:

+- will check for a single or multiple characters to the left.

```
re.search(r'Co+kie', 'Cooookie').group()
'Cooookie'
```

*- will check for either a zero or multiple characters to the left

will check for any occurrence of either 'a' or 'o' or both in the sequence in question.

```
re.search(r'Ca*o*kie', 'Cookie').group()
'Caokie'
```

? Will check for zero or a single character to the left

```
# Checks for exactly zero or one occurrence of a or o or both in the
given sequence
re.search(r'Colou?r', 'Color').group()
'Color'
```

That was easy, right? What about an instance where you would like to determine a given number of sequence repetition e.g. check the validity of a phone contact in some application? With the use of these regular expressions, the module-'re' will handle this with a lot of grace:

{x} means repeating x number of times

{x,} means repeating not less than x times (or more)

{x,y} means repeating not less than x times, but again, not more than y times.

```
re.search(r'\d{9,10}', '0987654321').group()
'0987654321'
```

The qualifiers * and + are, well, said to be 'greedy'.

Groups/Grouping Using Regular Expressions

Assume you are validating email addresses and have the desire to check the user name and host separately. This is exactly when the regular expressions 'group' feature comes in handy. It, for one, lets you pick up sections of the matching text.

Sections of a regular expression pattern enclosed by parenthesis are known as groups. Instead of changing what the expression matches, the parenthesis forms groups inside the matched sequence. Most examples in this regard use the 'group()' function but the 'match.group()' (plain) without any argument is still the whole usual matched text.

```
match = re.search(r'([w.-]+)@([\w.-]+)', _____)


if _____:

  print(match.group()) # The whole matched text

  print(match.group(1)) # The username (group 1)

  print(match.group(2)) # The host (group 2)
```

Greedy and Non-Greedy Matching

When we have a special character matching as much of the string or search sequence as possible, we say it is a greedy match, the normal regular expression behavior that is sometimes not desired:

```
pattern = "cookie"
sequence = "Cake and cookie"

heading  = r'<h1>TITLE</h1>'
re.match(r'<.*>', heading).group()
'<h1>TITLE</h1>'
```

The <.*> pattern matched the entire string, all the way to the second > occurrence. Nonetheless, if you just wanted to match the initial <hi> tag, you could just have used the greedy qualifier *? Which, as much as possible, matches very little text.

When you add ? after the qualifier, you make it perform the match in a minimal or non-greedy manner. This means that only as few as possible characters will match. Running <.*> only provides you a match with <h1>.

```
heading  = r'<h1>TITLE</h1>'
re.match(r'<.*?>', heading).group()
'<h1>'
```

The 're' Python Library

The re Python library offers a number of functions that make it a skill worth mastering. Chances are, you have seen some of them already like the re.match(), re.search(). We will now take a look at some useful functions in more detail:

search(pattern, string, flags=0)

This function allows you to scan through the given sequence or string to determine the first location whereby the RE is producing a match. It then returns a matching match object when it is found, else returns 'None' when no position in the string is matching the pattern. You need to note that 'None' is different from determining a zero length match in the string at some point.

```
pattern = "cookie"
sequence = "Cake and cookie"

re.search(pattern, sequence).group()
'cookie'
```

323

match(pattern, string, flags=0)

This one returns a corresponding/agreeing match object when zero or multiple characters at the start of the string are matching the pattern. Else in this case, returns 'None', if the string is not matching the pattern in question.

```
pattern = "C"
sequence1 = "IceCream"

# No match since "C" is not at the start of "IceCream"
re.match(pattern, sequence1)
sequence2 = "Cake"

re.match(pattern,sequence2).group()
'C'
```

search() and match()

The function 'match ()' checks for a match just at the beginning of the string—by default. The 'search()' function on the other hand checks for a match anywhere on the string.

findall(pattern, string, flags=0)

This one helps find the possible matches in the whole sequence and returns them as a strings' list. Every returned string denotes a single match.

```
email_address = "Please contact us at: manuelbee88@gmail.com, manuelbee88@gmail.com"

#'addresses' is a list that stores all the possible match

addresses = re.findall(r'[\w\.-]+@[\w\.-]+', email_address)

for address in addresses:

    print(address)
```

manuelbee88@gmail.com

manuelbee88@gmail.com

sub(pattern, repl, string, count=0, flags=0)

This one is the function 'substitute'; it returns the string acquired by replacing or even replacing the leftmost and non-overlapping pattern occurrences in string by the 'repl' replacement. If the pattern is actually identified, this means that the string is returned unaffected.

```
email_address = "Please contact us at: manuelbee88@gmail.com"

new_email_address        =        re.sub(r'([\w\.-]+)@([\w\.-]+)',        r'
manuelbee88@gmail.com', email_address)

print(new_email_address)
```

Please contact us at: manuelbee88@gmail.com

compile(pattern, flags=0)

This one compiles a pattern of regular expressions into a regular expressions object. In the instance you want to use an expression in one program multiple times, you can use the function 'compile()' to save the resultant regular expression object to reuse for purposes of efficiency. The reason behind this is simple: the compiled versions of the very current patterns passed to 'compile()' and module-level matching functions have been cached.

```
pattern = re.compile(r"cookie")
sequence = "Cake and cookie"
pattern.search(sequence).group()
'cookie'
# This is equivalent to:
re.search(pattern, sequence).group()
'cookie'
```

Just as a takeaway tip, you can modify the behavior of an expression by specifying the value of a 'flags'. In this case, you can add it (flag) as an additional argument to the various functions you know. Some of the flags include the following:

✓ DOTALL
✓ IGNORECASE
✓ MULTILINE
✓ VERBOSE

At this point, I believe you have seen how regular expressions work in Python. This is the perfect time to get our hands dirty:

Practical Exercise: How to Work with Regular Expressions

Let us look at a case study on how to work with regular expressions to put what you have learnt so far to work

```
import re
import requests
the_idiot_url = 'https://www.gutenberg.org/files/2638/2638-
0.txt'

def get_book(url):
    # Sends a http request to get the text from project Gutenberg
    raw = requests.get(url).text
    # Discards the metadata from the beginning of the book
    start = re.search(r"\*\*\* START OF THIS PROJECT
GUTENBERG EBOOK .* \*\*\*",raw ).end()
    # Discards the metadata from the end of the book
    stop = re.search(r"II", raw).start()
    # Keeps the relevant text
    text = raw[start:stop]
    return text

def preprocess(sentence):
    return re.sub('[^A-Za-z0-9.]+',' ', sentence).lower()


book = get_book(the_idiot_url)
processed_book = preprocess(book)
print(processed_book)
```

In the corpus, look for the number of the word 'the'. I will give you a hint: use the function 'len()'.

```
len(re.findall(r'the', processed_book))
302
```

In the corpus, try changing all the stand-alone i instances to I. just ensure you do not convert an 'i' that is occurring in a word-take a look:

```
processed_book = re.sub(r'\si\s', " I ", processed_book)
print(processed_book)
```

Look for the number of times anybody was quoted in the corpus (using "").

```
len(re.findall(r'\"', book))
96
```

In the corpus, which words are connected by the sign '--'?

```
re.findall(r'[a-zA-Z0-9]*--[a-zA-Z0-9]*', book)
['ironical--it',
 'malicious--smile',
 'fur--or',
 'astrachan--overcoat',
 'it--the',
 'Italy--was',
 'malady--a',
 'money--and',
 'little--to',
 'No--Mr',
 'is--where',
 'I--I',
 'I--',
 '--though',
 'crime--we',
 'or--judge',
 'gaiters--still',
 '--if',
 'through--well',
 'say--through',
 'however--and',
 'Epanchin--oh',
 'too--at',
 'was--and',
 'Andreevitch--that',
 'everyone--that',
 'reduce--or',
 'raise--to',
 'listen--and',
 'history--but',
 'individual--one',
 'yes--I',
 'but--',
 't--not',
 'me--then',
 'perhaps--',
 'Yes--those',
```

'me--is',
'servility--if',
'Roggin--hereditary',
'citizen--who',
'least--goodness',
'memory--but',
'latter--since',
'Roggin--hung',
'him--I',
'anything--she',
'old--and',
'you--scarecrow',
'certainly--certainly',
'father--I',
'Barashkoff--I',
'see--and',
'everything--Lebedeff',
'about--he',
'now--I',
'Lihachof--',
'Zaleshoff--looking',
'old--fifty',
'so--and',
'this--do',
'day--not',
'that--',
'do--by',
'know--my',
'illness--I',
'well--here',
'fellow--you']

Python Properties

Today, programmers usually consider creating getters and setters for the public properties of a class as best practice. In case you are wondering, getters and setters are simply methods that manage class attributes, thus increasing the attributes' safety even though coming at a cost of verbosity and simplicity. In Python, you can have it both ways.

Many languages will let you implement this in different methods, either with the use of a function such as 'person.getName ()' or with a language specific 'set' or 'get' construct. Python uses '@property' to do this.

In this chapter, we will be talking about the Python property decorator that you may have seen used with the syntax '@decorator':

```
class Person(object):
    def __init__(self, first_name, last_name):
        self.first_name = first_name
        self.last_name = last_name

    @property
    def full_name(self):
        return self.first_name + ' ' + self.last_name

    @full_name.setter
    def full_name(self, value):
        first_name, last_name = value.split(' ')
        self.first_name = first_name
        self.last_name = last_name

    @full_name.deleter
    def full_name(self):
        del self.first_name
        del self.last_name
```

This is how Python creates getters and setters, and deleters (also known as <u>mutator methods</u>). In this case, the decorator '@property' makes it this way so that you call the method 'full_name(self)' as though it is a normal property, while in reality, it is a method containing code to be run when the property gets set.

When you use a getter, setter, or deleter this way, it will provide you with a few advantages, some of which are below:

Validation: Before you set the internal property, you can try validating that the value provided is meeting some criteria, and if it does not, have it return an error.

It also provides <u>lazy loading</u>—resources can be loaded lazily to defer work until it is necessary to save time and resources.

Abstraction: The getters and setters let you abstract out the internal data representation. The example we looked at earlier, for instance, has the first name and last name stored separately. However, the getters and setters have the logic that creates a full name using the first and last names.

Debugging: the mutator methods can actually encapsulate any code and because of this, it is indeed a significant area for interception when logging or debugging code. For instance, you can inspect or log every time the value of a property changes.

To achieve this functionality, Python uses decorators. Decorators are special methods used to change the behavior or a different class or function. To illustrate how the decorator '@property' works, we will look at a simpler decorator as well as its internal workings. A decorator is also a function that assumes another function to be an argument, and wraps it to add it to its behavior. Look at the simple example below:

```
# decorator.py

def some_func():
    print 'Hey, you guys'

def my_decorator(func):
    def inner():
        print 'Before func!'
        func()
        print 'After func!'

    return inner

print 'some_func():'
some_func()

print ''

some_func_decorated = my_decorator(some_func)

print 'some_func() with decorator:'
some_func_decorated()
```

When you run this code, you get the following:

```
$ python decorator.py
some_func():
Hey, you guys

some_func() with decorator:
Before func!
Hey, you guys
After func!
```

You can see that the function 'my_decorator' is creating a new function dynamically to return with the input function, and adds code to be executed before the running of the original function and of course, after.

The decorator 'property' is implemented using a pattern that is similar to the function 'my_decorator'. When the syntax

'@decorator' is used, it gets the decorated function as the argument. See this in the example below:

some_func_decorated = my_decorator(some_func).

We will now go back to the first example with the code:

```
@property
def full_name_getter(self):
    return self.first_name + ' ' + self.last_name
```

Roughly, it is the same as the following:

```
def full_name_getter(self):
    return self.first_name + ' ' + self.last_name

full_name = property(full_name_getter)
```

(For purposes of better clarity, I changed a couple of function names)

Later on when you desire to use of '@full_name.setters' as the example describes, what we are really calling is:

```
def full_name_setter(self, value):
    first_name, last_name = value.split(' ')
    self.first_name = first_name
    self.last_name = last_name

full_name = property(full_name_getter)
full_name = full_name.setter(full_name_setter)
```

Well, this new object 'full_name' (being an instance of the object 'property') contains getter as well as setter methods.

To be able to use these in the 'person' class, the object 'property' has to act as the descriptor—this means that it contains its own methods including__get__(), __set__() and __delete__(). The methods __get__() and __set__() become triggered on an object when a property becomes retrieved or set, while the __delete__() method is triggered when a property gets deleted using 'del'.

Therefore, the __set__() method is triggered by 'person.full_name= Billy Bob'- this method is inherited from the 'object'. This clearly brings us to a very important point: for this to work, your class has to inherit from the 'object'. Therefore, a class such as this one would not be able to use the setter properties because it does not inherit from the'object' as follows:

```
class Person:
    pass
```

Thanks to 'property', these methods are now corresponding to the 'full_name_getter' as well as 'full_name_setter' methods.

```
full_name.fget is full_name_getter   # True
full_name.fset is full_name_setter   # True
```

The 'fset' and 'fget' are currently wrapped by both .__set__() and .__get__(). Lastly, you need to note that it is possible to access these descriptor objects by passing a reference to the 'person' class as follows:

```
>>> person = Person('Billy', 'Bob')
>>>
>>> full_name.__get__(person)
Billy Bob
>>>
>>> full_name.__set__(person, 'Timmy Thomas')
>>>
```

```
>>> person.first_name
Timmy
>>> person.last_name
Thomas
```

This is exactly how Python properties work beneath the surface.

Assert Handling in Python

In Python, the assert statement is actually a debugging aid that we use to test a condition. In the instance the condition happens to be true, it does not do anything and your program goes on to execute. However, if the assert condition has evaluated it as false, it raises an exception 'AssertionError' with the optional error message.

Assertions work best to inform you, the programmer, about unrecoverable errors in your program. The intent of these is not to signal expected error conditions such as 'file not found' in which case the user can just take a corrective action or simply try again.

Put differently, assertions are more like internal self-checks for your program that function by making declarations of some conditions in your code as impossible. In case one of these conditions does not hold, it means that the program has a bug.

This also means that if your program is bug free, these conditions can never occur. However, in case they occur, the program will definitely crash with an assertion error informing you about the triggered 'impossible' condition. This will make tracking down and fixing bugs in your programs much easier.

In case you need to simulate your code such as what is taking place in each stage, you can then use Python assert statements in the code.

Take a look at the basic structure of Python assert statements below:

The assert condition

To understand the flaw of your code better, you can send info with the assert statement. The following shows how you can give a message using the assert statement.

assert condition, your message

The assert statement

In Python, the assert statement takes a condition, and the condition has to be true. In case the condition is true, it means the value's assertion of the variable is okay and thus, the program will run smoothly and the subsequent statement will execute. However, if the condition is false, which means buggy code, it just raises an exception.

The assert example

You want to write a function that is going to return the quotient of two numbers. The code is as follows:

```
# defining the function definition
def divide(num1, num2):
    assert num2 > 0 , "Divisor cannot be zero"
    return num1/num2
# calling the divide function
a1 = divide(12,3)
# print the quotient
print(a1)
# this will give the assertion error
a2 = divide(12,0)
print(a2)
```

Running the code above gives you the following output:

4.0
Traceback (most recent call last):
  File "D:/T_Code/PythonPackage3/Assert.py", line 10, in
    a2 = divide(12,0)
  File "D:/T_Code/PythonPackage3/Assert.py", line 3, in divide
    assert num2>0 , "Divisor cannot be zero"
AssertionError: Divisor cannot be zero

If you check the third line of the code above, you will see the assert statement clearly. This is the line checked if the num2 variable is greater than zero or not. If it is greater than zero i.e. the condition is true, no problems will occur and the system will produce the output accordingly. However, when you called the 'division()' function with the second argument zero, it means the assert condition is seen to be false. This is exactly why there occurs an 'AssertionError' and a short message appears—this is 'divisor cannot be zero', which you wrote in the message section of the assert statement.

The assert example this time with variable replacement

Take the code below as an example, where you want to get the square root of the equation like b2-4ac.

```
import math
def sqrt(a,b,c):
    assert b*b >= 4*a*c, "Cannot find square root of negative
number, found %s < %s" % (b*b, 4*a*c)
    return math.sqrt(b*b - 4*a*c)

print(sqrt(10, 12, 3))
# this will cause assertion error
print(sqrt(-4, 5, -3))
```

The output is as follows:

```
4.898979485566356
Traceback (most recent call last):
  File "D:/T Code/PythonPackage3/Assert.py", line 20, in <module>
    print(sqrt(-4, 5, -3))
  File "D:/T Code/PythonPackage3/Assert.py", line 16, in sqrt
    assert b*b >= 4*a*c, "Cannot find square root of negative number, found %s < %s" % (b*b, 4*a*c)
AssertionError: Cannot find square root of negative number, found 25 < 48

Process finished with exit code 1
```

Below is a simple example that can help you gain a better understanding of where assertions could come in handy. I tried giving this one a bit more semblance of a real world issue you could actually come across in one of your programs.

Assume you are using Python to build an online store. You want to add a functionality of a discount coupon to the system and therefore write the function 'apply_discount':

```
def apply_discount(product, discount):
    price = int(product['price'] * (1.0 - discount))
    assert 0 <= price <= product['price']
    return price
```

You need to note the 'assert' statement in there. It guarantees you that regardless of what may occur, discounted prices cannot go below $0 and cannot go higher than the product's original price.

You need to make sure that is really working as intended if this function is called to implement a valid discount as follows:

```
#
# Our example product: Nice shoes for $149.00
#
>>> shoes = {'name': 'Fancy Shoes', 'price': 14900}

#
# 25% off -> $111.75
#
>>> apply_discount(shoes, 0.25)
11175
```

Oh well, that worked nicely. You now need to apply a couple of invalid discounts as follows:

```
#
# A "200% off" discount:
#
>>> apply_discount(shoes, 2.0)
Traceback (most recent call last):
  File "<input>", line 1, in <module>
    apply_discount(prod, 2.0)
  File "<input>", line 4, in apply_discount
    assert 0 <= price <= product['price']
AssertionError

#
# A "-30% off" discount:
#
>>> apply_discount(shoes, -0.3)
Traceback (most recent call last):
  File "<input>", line 1, in <module>
    apply_discount(prod, -0.3)
  File "<input>", line 4, in apply_discount
    assert 0 <= price <= product['price']
AssertionError
```

You can see very well that when you try applying an invalid discount, it raises an exception 'AssertionError' that essentially points out the line containing the violated assertion condition. If you ever encounter such an error as you test your online store, it will be simple to know what took place by looking at the traceback.

This is the power of Python assertions.

The Syntax

Studying up on the way Python implements a language feature is always a good idea— that is before you begin using it. That said, we shall now take a quick glance at the assert statement's syntax:

340

assert_stmt ::= "assert" expression1 ["," expression2]

'expression1' in this case refers to the condition you test while the 'expression2', which is optional, is an error message displayed in case the assertion fails. During the execution time, the Python interpreter will transform every assert statement into the following:

```
if __debug__:
  if not expression1:
    raise AssertionError(expression2)
```

You can simply pass an optional error message by using 'expression2'- the message will display in the traceback with the 'AssertionError'. This can simplify debugging even more. For instance, you might have seen code such as this one:

```
if cond == 'x':
  do_x()
elif cond == 'y':
  do_y()
else:
  assert False, ("This should never happen, but it does
occasionally. "
          "We're currently trying to figure out why. "
          "Email dbader if you encounter this in the wild.")
```

While this is undoubtedly ugly, its still a valid and useful method that will come in handy especially if you face an issue of heisenbug—type in any one of your programs.

Are There Drawbacks To The Use Of Asserts In Python?

Before we continue, you need to note that there are several caveats that come with the use of assertions in Python. Since

341

we do not have the luxury of discussing all of them, I will mention one of them.

This one has everything to do with bringing bugs and security risks to your applications.

Do not use asserts for Validation of data!

Asserts can be switched off in the interpreter. Do not rely on the assert expressions to execute for validation of data or processing of the same.

The fact that anyone on the planet can disable assertions stands as the biggest caveat. The -o and -oo command line switches and the environment variable PYTHONOPTIMIZE in CPython are used for this. This makes all assert statements null—operations and the assertion are just compiled away and do not get evaluated. This means that none of the conditional expressions will execute.

This is an intentional design decision used in the same way by other languages. The arising side effect is that it gets very dangerous to actually use the assert statements as a fast and simple way to actually validate input data. I will explain:

Suppose your program makes use of asserts to actually determine whether a function argument has an unexpected or 'wrong' value. This can backfire quite fast and bring about security holes or bugs. Consider the following example:

Assume you are creating an online store app. Somewhere in your code, you have a function to delete a product as per the request of the user:

```
def delete_product(product_id, user):
    assert user.is_admin(), 'Must have admin privileges to delete'
    assert store.product_exists(product_id), 'Unknown product id'
    store.find_product(product_id).delete()
```

Look at the function here closely. What would happen if someone disabled the assertions? In this function example, we have two serious issues brought about by the wrong use of assert statements:

1. Looking for admin privileges using assert statements is detrimental. If someone has disabled the assertions in the interpreter, this will turn into a null-op. This means any user will be able to delete products. The check for privileges does not even run and this introduces possible security problems and allows attackers to damage the data in your company or customers' online store. That is not good.

2. The disabling of assertions means the program skips the check 'product_exists ()'. This means that 'final_product ()' can now be called using invalid product ids. This could lead to severe bugs depending on how you have written the program. In the worst-case scenario, this could be a perfect avenue for a person to launch Denial of Service attacks against the store. The store app could crash if you attempted to delete an unknown product and thus, an attacker would be able to bombard it with multiple invalid delete requests and bring forth an outage.

How can you avert these issues? The answer is simple and plain: Do not use assertions for data validation. Instead, you could try doing your validation using regular if-statements and then raise validation exceptions if deemed necessary. For instance:

```
def delete_product(product_id, user):
  if not user.is_admin():
    raise AuthError('Must have admin privileges to delete')

  if not store.product_exists(product_id):
    raise ValueError('Unknown product id')

  store.find_product(product_id).delete()
```

This example also comes with the benefit that instead of raising undefined or vague AssertionError exceptions, it now raises exceptions that are semantically right such as ValueError or even AuthError.

Exception Handling in Python

So far, you know and appreciate that errors happen as we program. Programming bugs and errors are an unpleasant fact. Perhaps you gave bad input; perhaps a network resource was not available; perhaps the program's memory ran out, or you may have made a simple mistake while programming.

Exceptions are Python's solution to these errors, and I am sure you have seen an exception at least once before. Exception handling lets you handle errors with grace and do something about it in a meaningful way. To handle exception, the Python language uses try .. except .. block.

The syntax is as follows:

```
try:
  # write some code
  # that might throw exception
except <ExceptionType>:
  # Exception handler, alert the user
```

You need to write code that is likely to throw an exception as you can see in the try block. When exception takes place, the program skips the code in the try block. If a matching exception type exists in the except clause, it means its handler is executed.

We will look at an example here:

```
try:
  f = open('somefile.txt', 'r')
  print(f.read())
  f.close()
except IOError:
  print('file not found')
```

The code above works in the following way:

The first statement in between 'try' and 'except' executes. If there is no exception occurring, the program skips the code beneath clause.

If there is no file in existence, the program shall raise an exception and skips the other part of the code in the try. When the exception occurs, and the exception type is matching exception name after the except keyword, the code in the except clause executes.

You need to note that the code above is has the ability to handle IOError exception only. If you want to handle another type of exception, you will need to add additional except clause.

The try statement can actually now have more than one except clause, and it can have optional else or/and finally statement.

```
try:
   <body>
except <ExceptionType1>:
   <handler1>
except <ExceptionTypeN>:
   <handlerN>
except:
   <handlerExcept>
else:
   <process_else>
finally:
   <process_finally>
```

The clause is the same as elif. When an exception is occurring, it has to undergo a check checked in order to match the exception type in the except clause. If a match is present, it means handler for the matching case executes. You also need to note that ExceptionType is omitted in the last except clause. If the exception is not matching any exception type before the last except clause, the last except clause handler executes. Also note that the statements below the else clause only run when there is no exception raised.

Secondly, the statements in the finally block run all the time regardless of whether exception occur or not.

Let us now look at another example:

```
try:

  num1, num2 = eval(input("Enter two numbers, separated by a comma : "))

  result = num1 / num2

  print("Result is", result)


except ZeroDivisionError:

  print("Division by zero is error !!")


except SyntaxError:

  print("Comma is missing. Enter numbers separated by comma like this 1, 2")


except:

  print("Wrong input")


else:

  print("No exceptions")


finally:

  print("This will execute no matter what")
```

Please note that the function 'eval()' allows a python program to run Python code right within itself; the function expects what's referred to as a string argument. You can learn some more about eval() by visiting this <u>page</u>.

Raising Exceptions

To raise the exceptions from your own methods, you need to use the 'raise' keyword as follows in order:

raise ExceptionClass("Your argument")

Here is an example:

```
def enterage(age):
    if age < 0:
        raise ValueError("Only positive integers are allowed")

    if age % 2 == 0:
        print("age is even")
    else:
        print("age is odd")

try:
    num = int(input("Enter your age: "))
    enterage(num)

except ValueError:
    print("Only positive integers are allowed")
except:
    print("something is wrong")
```

You can now run the program and input a positive integer.

The expected output is as follows:

Enter your age: 12
age id even

Once again, run the program and input a negative integer.

The expected output is as follows:

Enter your age: -12

Only integers are allowed

The Use of Exceptional Objects

Now that you have an idea of handling exceptions, we will now learn what it really entails to handle exception object in exception handler code. You can use the code below to assign exception objects to variables.

```
try:
    # this code is expected to throw exception
except ExceptionType as ex:
    # code to handle exception
```

You can clearly see that you can be able to store exception object in the variable ex. You can now use this particular object in exception handler code.

```
try:
    number = eval(input("Enter a number: "))
    print("The number entered is", number)
except NameError as ex:
    print("Exception:", ex)
```

Now run the program and then input a number.

The expected output is as follows:

Enter a number: 34
The number entered is 34

Likewise, run the program and then key in a string.

The expected output is as follows:

Enter a number: one

Exception: name 'one' is not defined

Creating a Custom Exceptional Class

You can extend BaseException class or BaseException subclass to create your custom exception class. Look at the diagram below:

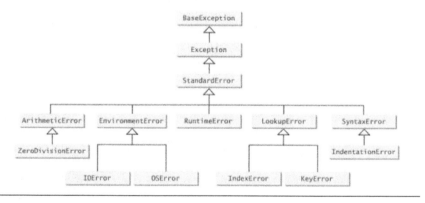

As you can clearly see, the majority of Python exception classes in Python are extending from the BaseException class. You can acquire your own exception class from BaseException class or BaseException subclass such as RuntimeError.

Just create a fresh file named NegativeAgeException.py and proceed to write the code below:

```python
lass NegativeAgeException(RuntimeError):
    def __init__(self, age):
        super().__init__()
        self.age = age
```

The code above builds a fresh exception class called NegativeAgeException made up of constructors alone that call the parent class constructor with super().__init__() and the age is set.

The use of custom exception class

```python
def enterage(age):
    if age < 0:
        raise NegativeAgeException("Only positive integers are allowed")

    if age % 2 == 0:
        print("age is even")
    else:
        print("age is odd")

try:
    num = int(input("Enter your age: "))
    enterage(num)
except NegativeAgeException:
    print("Only positive integers are allowed")
except:
    print("something is wrong")
```

Summing Things Up: Using Python and Django to Create a Simple Website

Today, you will learn how to create a functional website called iFriends. Even though this website is quite basic, it will form the basis for building something bigger as you get the guidance you need through the different Django framework aspects.

First off, let us define this strange term, Django.

What is Django?

Django is a free web application framework written in Python. A web framework is a set of components that aid in the development of websites in a quicker and easier way.

When you are building a website, you require a set of components that are similar—that is a way to handle user authentication—that entails signing up, in, and signing out, your website's management panel, forms, and among other things, a way to upload the files.

Because web developers tend to face the same problems when building a new site, a good number of them teamed up and came up with frameworks such as Django to offer ready-made components.

The Purpose of a Framework like Django

To understand what Django is actually for, you will need to take a better look at the servers. Essentially, the server has to

352

know, as the first thing, that you need it to serve you a web page.

Take a mailbox monitored for requests or incoming letters as an example. A webserver is responsible for this. This web server will read the letter and then relay a rejoinder with a webpage. However, when you want to send something, you need to have some content; Django is what helps you create that content.

What occurs when a person requests a website from your server?

In the instance a request comes to a web server, it goes to Django, which then tries to make out the request in reality. It first picks the address from a web page and tries to understand what to do. This 'urlresolver' in Django complete the section (you need to note that in this case, URL 'Uniform Resource Locator' is a web address, which is why the name urlresolver is making sense).

Well, that is not very smart. It gets a list of patterns and tries matching the URL. Django checks the patterns from top to bottom; if something matches, Django simply passes the request to 'view', which is the associated function.

Try to imagine a mail carrier carrying a letter. He walks down the streets checking each number against the one written on the letter. When he notes a match, she places the letter there. That is how the urlresolver operates.

In the function 'view', every interesting thing is done; you can check the database in search for some details. Perhaps the user requested to change something contained in the data. Maybe like a letter stating 'change my job description'. The 'view' can check whether you can do that, and then update the description of the job and send a message back as follows:

'done!' The 'view' then generates a response and at this point, Django can relay it to the user's web browser.

Without a doubt, the above description is a bit simplified. However, if you ask me, you do not need to know all the technical workings yet. Just have the general idea first for now.

Rather than go too much into the details, we will just start using Django to create something cool and learn all you need to know along the way.

A Django Project

This simply refers to a collection of settings that define a particular Django instance. The settings usually include things like URL configuration, database configuration as well as various other options, which you will learn as you go along.

It is relatively simple to create a Django project from the command prompt. Just follow the steps below:

Change the directory (from the command prompt) where you need to store your code for the iFriends project.

Build a directory known as iFriends, which will be the root directory for this project.

Now change to this directory (iFriends).

Type the command below to create the project:

```
python django-admin.py startproject iFriends
```

NOTE: Since the project will be a Python package, you should avoid using a project name that may be in conflict with any current in-built packages in Python. You can see the documentation for the in-built Python packages here.

Secondly, you do not need to place your project code in a directory in the document base of the web server. The Django framework is always responsible for executing such code. Actually, you will find it a better idea to keep the code some place outside the root of the web server so that your code remains protected from direct access from a web browser.

The command 'startproject' first creates a directory known as iFriends and then stores the basic Python files required to start the project in the directory. The 'startproject' command creates the files below:

✓ The empty file '__init__.py' that informs Python that the website directory needs to be treated like a Python package.

✓ The command line utility 'manage.py', which lets the administrator start and manage the Django project.

✓ The configuration file 'settings.py' that controls the Django project behavior.

✓ Python file 'urls.py', which defines the syntax and then configures the URLs' behavior, which will come in handy in accessing the website.

These files have a basic purpose: setting up a Python package, which Django can actually use to define the structure as well as behavior of a website. As the website grows in complexity, we will discuss more of this.

Start the development server

Once you have created the Django project, you have to be able to begin the development server so that you test it. A development server is a webserver that comes with the Django project. This server allows you to develop your website without worrying about dealing with issues of configuration and management of a production web server.

To start your development server, you need to do the following:

Change the root directory from the command prompt for the project 'iFriends'.

Enter the command line below to start the development server.

python manage.py runserver

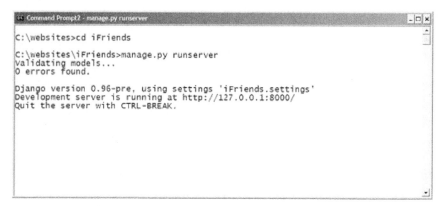

```
Command Prompt2 - manage.py runserver                          _ □ ×

C:\websites>cd iFriends

C:\websites\iFriends>manage.py runserver
Validating models...
0 errors found.

Django version 0.96-pre, using settings 'iFriends.settings'
Development server is running at http://127.0.0.1:8000/
Quit the server with CTRL-BREAK.
```

NOTE: The command 'createproject' that we discussed about earlier copies the utility 'manage.py' into your project's root. This utility initially validates the project and then reports all errors. In case there are no critical errors encountered, you receive a notification that the development server is running at http://127.0.0.1:8000/.

Now verify that your development server is functioning as expected—open a web browser and enter the address below:

http://127.0.0.1:8000/

In case the development server begins correctly—and you do not have the debug setting changed—you will see a page like the one described below:

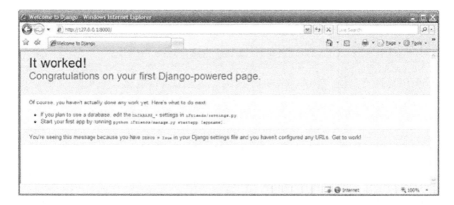

NOTE: You can inform the development server to use a different port apart from 8000 if that one is already in use. You can so this by adding a port to the command line. Below is an example showing the syntax for the configuration for the development server to run on port 8008:

```
manage.py runserver 8008
```

Secondly, I hope you know that if you want to stop the development server, you can simply press Ctrl+ Break or instead, Ctrl+C.

Configure the database

Once you have verified that you can actually stop and start the development server, you need to configure access to the database. We will now look at the process of making and configuring access to the database that we will use in the sample project.

NOTE: Django can serve web pages dynamically without the need for a database for the storage of information. Nonetheless, I would say that one of the best features in Django is the ability to actually implement website backed by database.

The configuration process involves three steps:

1. Creating the database and assigning the rights

2. Modifying the file 'settings.py' to specify the type, location, name and access credentials of the database.

3. Synchronizing the Django project with the database to build the initial tables required for the Django engine.

Django supports a number of different database engine types. In this book, we will use a MySQL database for the project. My assumption is that you have installed, configured, and already started a database engine that you can access from the development server.

NOTE: MySQL database doesn't let you use any names that are case sensitive whenever creating tables. In case you would like to define objects in a project that has uppercase characters, you will have to turn off case sensitivity in the Django framework. To do this, you can use the setting below contained in the file '<django installation:

```
path>/django/db/backends/__init__.py'

uses_case_insensitive_names = True
```

Creating database and granting rights

We will now learn how to create the database, an admin user, and about granting different rights from the SQL database command console. Also, we will learn how to modify the setting 'uses_case_insensitive_names' within the Django framework to enable you to label objects using the uppercase characters. Do the following:

Enter the command line below from the SQL database command console to create an 'iFriends' database:

CREATE DATABASE iFriendsDB

To start using the database, enter the command below:

USE iFriendsDB

To create an administrative user with the name dAdmin, enter the command below with a password called test:

CREATE USER 'dAdmin'@'localhost' IDENTIFIED BY 'test'

Enter the command below to grant all the rights on the database (iFriends) to the dAdmin user:

GRANT ALL ON *.* TO 'dAdmin'@'localhost'

NOTE: In case the database engine has any graphical interface, which lets you manage databases as well as users, you can also try using that interface to create the database, admin user, as well as to assign rights.

Now open the file

'<Django installation path>/Django/db/backbends/__init__.py' in your editor.

Add the setting below to the file so that the MySQL database case sensitivity is disabled:

uses_case_insensitive_names = True

Save the file '__init__.py'

How to configure Database access in 'settings.py'

Once the database is up and running and you have a user account already set up for Django, you have to configure the 'settings.py' in the Django project to be able to have access to that database. Every Django project has a 'settings.py' file. The file 'settings.py' is a Python script, which actually configures different project settings.

Django uses the settings below in the 'settings.py' file to be able to control access to the database:

DATABASE_ENGINE (type of database engine). Django accepts the following:

postgresql_psycopg2, ado_mssql, mysql_old, mysql, sqlite3 and postgresql.

DATABASE_NAME

DATABASE_USER- this is the user account used as you connect to the database. With SQLite, no user is used.

DATABASE_PASSWORD- this refers to the password for the DATABASE_USER.

DATABASE_HOST- this refers to the host on which the database is stored. For localhost, you can leave this empty.

DATABASE_PORT- this is the port we use to connect to the database. If you are using the default port, you can leave this one empty.

Configuring Django to access the Database (iFriends)

We will now look at the steps you need to take to modify the file 'settings.py' settings for the database and user created in the last section— the MySQL database called iFriendsDB, and a dAdmin username with a password of test running on the default port and localhost.

In your text editor, open the file 'iFriends\settings.py':

Get the setting- DATABASE_ENGINE and then change the value to:

DATABASE_ENGINE = 'mysql'

Change the DATABASE_NAME setting value to:

DATABASE_NAME = 'iFriendsDB'

Change the DATABASE_USER setting value to:

DATABASE_USER = 'dAdmin'

Change the DATABASE_PASSWORD setting value to:

DATABASE_PASSWORD = 'test'

Verify that the settings: DATABASE_PORT and DATABASE_HOST do not have a value:

DATABASE_HOST = '' and;

DATABASE_PORT = ''

NOTE: When DATABASE_PORT and DATABASE_HOST settings remain blank, they default to localhost and default port. In case the database is on a remote server, or maybe it is running on a non-default port, you need to set these options accordingly.

Synchronize the project to the Database

Once you have configured the database access in the file

'settings.py', you can now have your project synchronized to the database. The process of Django's synchronization will create the necessary tables in the database to support your project.

The creation of the tables will be according to the applications specified in the setting: 'INSTALLED_APPS' of the file 'settings.py'. Below include the default settings specified in the setting 'INSTALLED_APPS':

```
INSTALLED_APPS = (
  'django.contrib.auth',
  'django.contrib.contenttypes',
  'django.contrib.sessions',
  'django.contrib.sites',
)
```

Look at the list below describing the default applications installed in the Django project:

✓ The default authentication system that comes with Django- django.contrib.auth

✓ The types of content framework - django.contrib.contenttypes

✓ The framework which is utilized in the management of sessions- django.contrib.sessions

✓ The framework that is utilized in the management of many sites with one Django installation- django.contrib.sites

Synchronize the project 'iFriends ' to the iFriends Database

In this section, you will learn all the steps you need to go through to synchronize the Django project to the database.

362

During this process, Django builds the default tables then follows to prompt you so as to enter the email address, password, and name for the website admin account. The password and username you specify let you access the authentication system in Django.

Just ensure you have pressed Ctrl+ Break (from the console prompt) to stop the development server.

Change the iFriends project root directory

Enter the command below at the console prompt to start the synchronization as the image below illustrates:

python manage.py syncdb

```
Command Prompt2                                                    _ □ x
C:\websites\iFriends>python manage.py syncdb
Creating table auth_message
Creating table auth_group
Creating table auth_user
Creating table auth_permission
Creating table django_content_type
Creating table django_session
Creating table django_site

You just installed Django's auth system, which means you don't have any superuse
rs defined.
Would you like to create one now? (yes/no): y
Please enter either "yes" or "no": yes
Username: django
E-mail address: django@iFriends.com
Password:
Password (again):
Superuser created successfully.
Installing index for auth.Message model
Installing index for auth.Permission model
Loading 'initial_data' fixtures...
No fixtures found.
```

(The image above shows synchronization of the initial Django project from a command line with the database)

Enter username at the prompt for the account of the website administrator.

Enter a password at the prompt for the account of the website administrator.

At this point, the database has the right tables configured to let Django use its content, authentication, session, and site frameworks right.

Install an application

Once you have configured as well as synchronized a given database, you can start installing apps on it. Installing apps is just a matter of building an application directory and defining a model, as well as activating the app to allow Django to have access to it in the database.

1: Build the first application

Try building an application called 'people' that we will utilize to track the people using the website as follows:

Change the root directory of the project 'iFriends' from the console prompt.

Type the command below in to make a blank application referred to as 'people':

```
python manage.py startapp People
```

The command 'startup' will create a directory 'people' inside the directory 'iFriends' and then populate it with the files below:

'__init__.py' is an important file for the use of apps as a Python package.

The Python code defining the model is contained in 'models.py'

The Python code defining the views for the model is contained in 'views.py'

PYTHON PROGRAMMING FOR ADVANCED

The file in the directory of the application defines how the app info will get stored and accessed in the database. Moreover, they define the way the information in the model will appear— and seen—as it is being accessed from the website.

2: Create a model

Once the application has been created, you will need to build a model for the data to be stored in the app. A model is a definition of the attributes, classes, and relationships of the objects in the app.

Creating a model is simple; just modify the file 'model.py' that is located in the app directory. The file 'models.py' is a script in Python used to define the tables that are to be included in the database for the storage of objects in the model.

At first, the file 'model' contains only a single line, which imports the object 'models' frin the package 'django.db'. You will need to define either or multiple classes so as to define the model. In the database, each class usually represents a given object type.

3: Creating a model for the application 'people'

We are now going to build the 'person' class in the model 'people' by making some modifications to 'models.py', the Python script for the application 'people'. At first, you will find that the script is blank. In this section, I will take you through adding the code in Python for the definition of classes in the model. Just:

Open the file 'iFriends\People\models.py' in your editor.

Open the command line below to the file in order to import the Django package 'models' into the application as follows:

from django.db import models

Now add the code snippet below to define the class 'Person' with email, name, and text attributes and headshot as follows:

1. class Person(models.Model):
2.   name = models.CharField('name', maxlength=200)
3.   email = models.EmailField('Email', blank=True)
4.   headshot = models.ImageField(upload_to='img', blank=True)
5.   text = models.TextField('Desc', maxlength=500, blank=True)
6.   def __str__(self):
7.   return '%s' % (self.name)

Now save the file.

You can see the full code for the file 'iFriends\People\models,py'.

from django.db import models

```
class Person(models.Model):
  name = models.CharField('name', max_length=200)
  text = models.TextField('Desc', max_length=500, blank=True)

  def __str__(self):
    return '%s' % (self.name)
```

NOTE: The '__str__' definition defines the object's string representation that can be used in views or other scripts in Python. Django uses the method __str__ severally for the display of objects as well.

4: Activate the model 'Person'

In this section, we will go through the process of activating the model 'person' by adding it to the setting 'INSTALLED_APPS' located in the file 'settings.py' before synchronizing the database. Just:

Open the file 'iFriends\settings.py' in your editor

Get the setting INSTALLED_APPS and then add the application 'iFriends.People' to it as you can see in the snippet below:

```
1.  INSTALLED_APPS = (
2.     'django.contrib.auth',
3.     'django.contrib.contenttypes',
4.     'django.contrib.sessions',
5.     'django.contrib.sites',
6.     'iFriends.People',
7.  )
```

Now save the file.

Synchronize this application (iFriends) into the database with the command below from the iFriends project root as shown in the figure below:

python manage.py syncdb

```
C:\websites\iFriends>python manage.py syncdb
Creating table People_person
Loading 'initial_data' fixtures...
No fixtures found.

C:\websites\iFriends>
```

The command 'syncdb' creates the appropriate tables in the database 'iFriends' for the application 'People'. At this point, the model is active and data can be added to the database and retrieved from the same with Django.

5: Using the API to add data

You will now learn how to make use of the Django shell interface as well as the API database to enable you to add a one 'Person' object to the people table quickly. This shell is a Python shell offering access to database API that is involved with Django. Your database API is a set of methods in Python that let you access the project database from this data model.

Add an object 'Person' to the iFriends database

After opening the Django shell, follow the steps below to have yourself added as an object 'Person' in the model 'People' of the database 'iFriends'.

Change the root directory of your project 'iFriends' from a console prompt.

Type the command below for the Django shell to be invoked:

python manage.py shell

Enter the code below from the shell prompt so that the 'Person' class is imported from the package 'people'.

```
from iFriends.People.models import Person
```

Type the command below to have an object 'Person' created called 'p'

```
p = Person(name="<your name>", email="<your eMail>")
```

Now save the object 'person' you have created with the command below:

p.save()

Confirm that the object was made with the function 'Person.objects.all()' that returns a list of the entire 'Person' objects and then print the list as follows:

```
lst = Person.objects.all()
print lst
```

The commands include the following:

```
Command Prompt2 - python manage.py shell                         _ □ x
C:\websites\iFriends>python manage.py shell
Python 2.4.2 (#67, Sep 28 2005, 12:41:11) [MSC v.1310 32 bit (Intel)] on win32
Type "help", "copyright", "credits" or "license" for more information.
(InteractiveConsole)
>>> from iFriends.People.models import Person
>>> p = Person(name="Brad Dayley", email="dayleybooks@yahoo.com")
>>> p.save()
>>> lst = Person.objects.all()
>>> print lst
[<Person: Brad Dayley>]
>>>
```

The object 'Person' has now been made in the database 'iFriends'.

6: Set up the file 'URLConf'

Here we will talk about the configuration of the file 'URLConf' to explain how the installed applications get accessed from the web. This file is a script that lets you define particular views accessed according to the sent URL (by the browser). On receiving a URL request, the Django server parses the request according to the patterns contained in the file 'URLConf'. In Python, this request is translated into a certain function that is executed in the file 'views.py', which we will discuss shortly.

NOTE: The 'URLConf' file location is defined by the setting 'ROOT_URLCONF' located in the file 'settings.py'. The default location is the project's root directory name. With regards to the project 'iFriends', the ROOT_URLCONF's value would be set to the value below, in which the 'iFriends.urls' is equivalent to 'iFriends/urls.py':

ROOT_URLCONF = 'iFriends.urls'

7: Add a URL pattern for a 'People' view use

In the example here, you will modify the setting 'urlpatterns' in the file 'iFriends/urls.py' to set up a small URL pattern for the application 'People'.

In your editor, open the file 'iFriends\urls.py'.

Find the setting 'urlpatterns' then add the pattern 'iFriends.People.views.index' to it as follows:

```
urlpatterns = patterns(",
(r'^People/$', 'iFriends.People.views.index')
)
```

Now save the file.

NOTE: The earlier code snippet 'iFriends.People.views.index' is referring to the function 'index()' that is located in the file 'iFriends/People/views.py' that we will discuss next.

8: Build a simple view

Having configured the file 'URLConf', you have to add the views to the application. The views of the application are stored in the file 'views.py' as functions in the application directory. When the Django servers get a URL request, it parses the request according to the patterns contained in the file

'URLConf' before determining the function to execute in order to generate the web view.

9: Now build the Index View for the application 'people'

The steps for building an index view of stub for the application 'People' in the project 'iFriends' are simple. Once the view is made, you begin the development server and view the generated web page. Just do the following:

Open the file 'iFriends/People/views.py' in your editor. The file 'views.py' is empty in the beginning. Add the code snippet below to the file using the editor.

```
from django.shortcuts import HttpResponse
from iFriends.People.models import Person

def index(request):
    html = "<H1>People</H1><HR>"
    return HttpResponse(html)
```

Now save the file.

Change the 'iFriends' project root directory from a command prompt.

Type the command below to begin the development server:

python manage.py runserver

Access the URL 'http://127.0.0.1:8000/People' to see a webpage that looks like this:

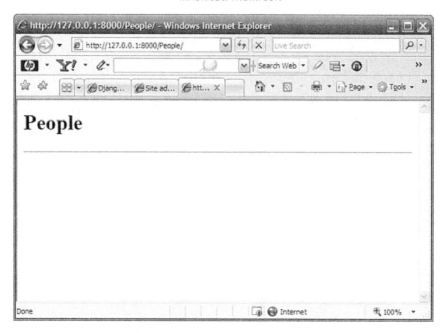

Recap

In this exercise, we made a Django project titled 'iFriends'. For the project, you configured access to the MySQL database. You also made an application known as 'People' then added a class 'Person' before populating the database with a single object 'Person'. After that, you configured the URL behavior in order to support an index view before adding the appropriate code in the view to display the objects' list in the class 'Person'.

I am sure all the steps we covered in this exercise have demonstrated to you how simple it is to create a website using the Django framework and Python. As your Python programming skills continue to develop, you should be able to build on this framework to implement a full-featured website.

Questions you might ask

How would I modify a model once it has synchronized to the database?

Django cannot be depended on to update models very reliably. If you want the easiest and safest way to modify an existing model, consider making changes to the model and then deleting all tables associated with it in the database with the SQL drop command, and lastly, use the command 'syncdb' to synchronize the model with the database.

Are there some means I can use to check for errors in the model before I try synchronizing to the database?

Django has some utility you can use to validate the contents of models before it synchronizes to the database. From the project's root directory, jus enter the following:

Python manage.py validate

The "validate utility" will then check the syntax of the model as well as logic and report any problems.

Conclusion

We have come to the end of the book. Thank you for reading and congratulations for reading until the end.

Well, that is all we had to cover. Congratulations for completing our Python series! I would really want to say that this is the end but unfortunately (or fortunately), it is not.

While we may have covered most relevant topics in Python, you still would need to go ahead and advance your knowledge in a good number of them. You will note that some will require a bit more research to learn more or prop and consolidate what you already know so far.

In this edition, we covered the following topics:

✓ File Management in Python

✓ Iterators in Python

✓ Python generators

✓ Intertools in Python

✓ Closures in Python Regular Expressions (RE)Python properties

✓ Assert and Exception handling in Python

✓ Summing things up: creating your own simple website with Python and Django

I hope you had fun and a great learning experience. All the best as you continue growing your Python programming skills:

If you found the book valuable, can you recommend it to others? One way to do that is to post a review on Amazon.

Click here to leave a review for this book on Amazon!

Thank you and good luck!

Printed in Great Britain
by Amazon

73620452R10214